money
magic

money magic

Unleashing Your True Potential for Prosperity and Fulfillment

Deborah L. Price

NEW WORLD LIBRARY
NOVATO, CALIFORNIA

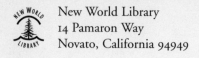

New World Library
14 Pamaron Way
Novato, California 94949

Front cover design by Mary Ann Casler
Text design and typography by Tona Pearce Myers

Library of Congress Cataloging-in-Publication Data
Price, Deborah L.
  Money magic : Unleashing your true potential for prosperity and fulfillment / by Deborah L. Price.
    p.   cm.
ISBN-10: 1-57731-244-9   ISBN-13: 978-1-57731-244-4
1. Finance, Personal — Psychological aspects. 2. Money — Psychological aspects. I. Title.
HG179.P7354 2000
332.024'01—dc21   00-056089

Previously published as *Money Therapy.*

First Paperback Printing, January 2003
ISBN 1-57731-244-9
Printed in Canada on acid-free, partially recycled paper
Distributed to the trade by Publishers Group West

10 9 8 7 6 5 4

This book is dedicated to my daughter,
Anjelica Price-Rocha, for the love,
beauty, and wisdom she has brought into
my life, and in loving memory of my friend,
Barbara Lossos, whose spirit is with us still.

contents

acknowledgments

It took a village to write this book. I am blessed to have an amazing community of friends, family, and colleagues who have encouraged and supported me in my efforts to write this book. With gratitude and thanks, I acknowledge each of you. I would like to specifically acknowledge:

My agent, Sheree Bykofsky, and Janet Rosen for believing in this book in the first place.

My editor, Georgia Hughes, and everyone at New World Library for their efforts in making this book possible.

Carol Weser, for being my eyes when I couldn't see.

Charlotte and Rodney Strong, for the gift of my life at Toad Hollow.

My daughter, Anjelica, for her immense patience and understanding.

The Wild Women of Healdsburg for all those Friday nights that saved me.

James Black and Julie Simons, for their care and feeding.

My wonderful friends and family — Marge Abrams, Brenda Ferreira, Elizabeth Harlow, Leslie Gainer, Marian Morioka, Mary Rubio, Carol Bell, Molly Light, Benjamin Schick, Caite Mathis, Julie Greenwalt, Kris Cuneo, Randy Price, Stephanie Skidmore, and Bob Rembowski — I love you all.

My mother, Pat Price, and my sister, Tricia Davisson, for their love and faith in me.

Sandy Plone, for the foreword of this book and for being my dear friend.

My clients who have stood by me and supported me through my life's many changes. I am grateful.

Peace and blessings to every one of you.

foreword

This wonderful book, *Money Magic,* represents a new tool to help individuals reconstruct their financial lives through the perspective of their spiritual development. Deborah Price has honed her knowledge, beliefs, and concepts into an amazing blend of expertise, in order to guide and educate others toward their highest potential. It is an outstanding contribution to the field, and those who have the courage to read and use its wisdom will benefit.

Many authors have written about prosperity — including about how success, power, fame, and money are interrelated with spirituality. As a clinical psychologist, I have learned from my clients' (and my own) struggles and conflicts what a core issue money represents in our psyches, our relationships, and in all aspects of our lives.

My first contact with Deborah Price was as my financial

consultant, and subsequently, a dear friend. Her wisdom, dedication to helping her clients, and integrity, which transcends that of most people in the business world, are apparent. She began the task of educating me about financial matters, gradually guiding me from "innocence" into accepting responsibility for my financial life. My journey had been dedicated to helping others heal childhood wounds and master the complexities of modern life. We both became acutely aware of the overlap between financial consulting, psychology, and the spiritual path we shared.

Money seems to represent the ultimate taboo! Many authors and therapists alike agree that people find it easier to reveal sexual confidences, for example, than to speak of money matters. Yet the power of early experiences and deeply held beliefs about money is clear. When individuals explore their treasured myths, conscious or unconscious, it becomes possible to better understand blocks or patterns that guide their financial decisions. Money can be a symbol in families for love as well as a symbol for violence. It may be used as a weapon in relationships, manipulating conflicts about sex, love, or power. Husbands and wives, parents and children, siblings — we're all prey to anger, envy, love, compassion, or worries about money in these complex relationships.

Having a harmonious relationship with one's finances is part of the mind/body/spirit connection to living a balanced and healthy life, and the prosperity principle is an attitude about life. A consciousness of abundance can become a self-fulfilling prophecy, as can a consciousness of scarcity. When clients ask how they might accomplish this shift, I encourage them to find a trustworthy advisor, to read available books on the subject, and to illuminate, understand, and then remove destructive myths or childhood beliefs that may block the path to prosperity.

Deborah Price has integrated sound psychological principles and universal spiritual beliefs with her extensive knowledge of financial planning in an easily readable, articulate form. Therapists will be recommending this book to couples as part of premarital counseling to help prevent later conflicts, and to young and mature individuals alike for a journey of self-discovery toward a peaceful and prosperous life.

— Sondra Plone, Ph.D.
Clinical Psychologist
Los Angeles, California

introduction

Man is born free; and everywhere he is in chains.
— Rousseau, *The Social Contract*, 1762

Today, in the wealthiest country in the world, our society is permeated with symptoms of fear and anxiety about money. These feelings affect both the rich and poor and bind us together more than we realize. Although the symptoms are different for each person, almost everyone suffers from some form of money-related stress. In 2001, our money issues became even more magnified with the unprecedented rise and fall of the stock market, creating worldwide recession and affecting the lives of billions of people. I do not believe this global "recess" is an accident. Given our precarious human condition, it is more likely a

cosmic "time-out;" a time to give birth to a new way of seeing and experiencing money; a time to change our financial
destiny; a time of revelation. The word *revelation* has two
distinctly different meanings. One is the unveiling of an
opportunity that is rich and magical; the other, in dark con-
trast, is quite simply, apocalyptic. The choice is ours. We
have experienced enough pain around money; it is time to
experience the magic and the joy. We must be willing, however, to see and do things differently.

I love life and people immensely and have always held
great hope in my heart for humanity. In the last few years,
however, I have been so profoundly alarmed and disturbed
by the state of the world that it has become increasingly difficult to remain a silent witness. In my work as a financial
advisor and money coach, I have seen people who are caught
up in the struggle to acquire more and more material possessions and experiencing an ever-growing sense of hope-
lessness and financial despair. People come to me seeking
"financial security" and searching for something more
meaningful in their lives.

Unfortunately, "more" often means a new car, a boat, a
bigger house, some *thing* that only serves to increase their
burden and further complicate their lives. Repeatedly, I have
watched people become enslaved by their insatiable need for
more things, so much so that their life's energy becomes
depleted. I do not make this statement with any judgment.
Rather, I believe we have been living in a consumer coma for
too long and that this mass unconsciousness greatly affects
our psyches and the world around us. We have become so
numb to the reality of what is really happening that we are

paralyzed to take action and make the changes necessary to sustain our lives on this planet.

The advertising and media industries have convinced us that we are nothing without money and material possessions. We are in the grips of a national obsession. We have been brainwashed into believing that material possessions are what we're supposed to want, that fulfillment comes from what we have rather than how we live and feel. At a time when we are running out of land to build more shopping malls, television and the Internet have created virtual shopping malls that allow us to shop twenty-four hours a day — all to fill a void that we deeply feel but fail to understand. Meanwhile, the billions of dollars we spend exploiting our mass addiction for buying things we don't really need could be used to save the Earth as it teeters on the edge of disaster.

Consumerism is the addiction of our time, and it is time we owned up to it because we have far too much to lose. I wrote *Money Magic* to help you remember the purpose of your life: the original purpose. The one you were born to live. You were not born to shop. You were not born to live your life indebted to the things you own. You were not meant to spend your life's energy working so that you could simply accumulate material possessions. That is not what prosperity and abundance are about.

Money is a tool meant to help transform your life in more meaningful ways. As a tool, it will facilitate the path of true fulfillment that comes from living your life intentionally and with purpose. It does not matter how much money you have if all you are doing is spending it to accumulate more things. This kind of spending is a waste of your life's energy. You were meant for far greater things, and within you resides a far greater truth. It is this truth that I hope you will rediscover. You have the power within you to manifest a more purposeful and prosperous life. You also have the power to choose to make a difference. We must all wake up and become part of the solution. For it is entirely possible that we are playing the final round of the money game called "all or nothing." Waking up is not easy, but in my experience, when we fail to hear the alarm, we are often in for a rude awakening.

My Wake-up Call

Eight years ago, the world as I knew it literally fell apart. On January 17, 1994, the Northridge earthquake hit Los Angeles. I had a premonition that it was coming. The day before I invited an architect friend to visit me, and asked him to evaluate the apartment building I was living in to see if it would hold up to a major earthquake. He humored me and checked out the building, saying it looked pretty sound and that it should hold up quite well. At approximately 4:00 A.M. the next morning, the earthquake hit. I was already awake. It felt and sounded like a bomb had hit us. I ran across the hall to grab my baby girl in the darkness and chaos. A few minutes later another earthquake hit, and we could hear the building beginning to split at the seams.

My husband and I, fearing for our lives, decided to get out of our third-floor apartment. We found our way to the front door only to discover we were locked in. It was pitch black, electric sparks hissed and flew around the room, and the smell of gas began to fill the air. I crawled on my hands and knees in the dark, frantically searching for my keys. As I waded through the glass and debris, my mind was flooded with fearful thoughts. Was this the end? Would we survive? My keys were nowhere to be found. I was not ready to die. As I thought of my baby, I grew determined to find a way out.

Then, out of the corner of my eye, I saw the glimmer of my keys lying in a heap of rubble. They were easily two hundred feet from the table I had placed them on. I crawled back to the front door and unlocked it, and we ran down the stairs to our neighbors. Together, with our children in tow, we and our neighbors drove down Montana Avenue, one of the wealthiest neighborhoods in the world, which now looked like a war zone. The sky was an eerie greenish black. All the signals had stopped working, and the streetlights were out. Slowly, we caravanned down the road, following our friends to the shelter of their parents' home, where we sat through what was the coldest, darkest night of my life. Huddled together in the living room, we cried and waited, wondering what the world would look like in the dawn.

Three days after the earthquake, I packed up my family and left Los Angeles to rebuild my life. Both my home and business were condemned. There was little left to salvage. I never went back to the apartment. I couldn't bear to see it again. Few of my friends or family could understand how I could leave my entire life behind without even knowing where I was going. It was okay with me that I didn't know. I knew the earthquake was my wake-up call, intended to shake me out of the life I had been living and discover the life I was meant to live.

Over the past few years, I had received signs and messages telling me I was not where I was supposed to be. I was unhappy with life in the city. The smog, the traffic, and the crime were all beginning to get to me. I longed for a simpler life. When my daughter was born, my desire to escape the city grew even stronger. After the earthquake, I could no longer go home or go to work; I felt it was time to surrender to God's plan. When we left, I only knew I was supposed to head north and have faith. The rest would be revealed to me in time.

Now, years later, I believe that the earthquake, while a terrifying experience, was a blessing in disguise. I did not lose anything that could not be recovered or that I could not live without. Even after the earthquake I experienced many more losses, more "aftershocks." I now see this part of my life as a long phase of learning to let go. The more I let go, the more room I had for what I truly needed and the more receptive I became to living my life's purpose.

Today, I live in the country surrounded by nature and tranquility. In the stillness of this space, my mind became quiet, and for the first time since I was a child, I could hear the voice within me and all that it needed to say. I learned that everything that falls apart comes together again. Our lives are like great mosaics. When we take the time to stand back and look at them, we see that every piece fits perfectly and beautifully together. The same is true of your life. This book will help you examine the pieces of your life in a new way. It will help you to become clearer about who you are and what you truly value. When you create the mosaic of your life, money should be part of the frame, not the picture.

Exploring Our Relationship to Money

Money possesses an energy and life of its own. It contains a duality similar to that present in our own nature. It is both spiritual and material, creative and destructive, loving and cruel. It can help us fulfill our greatest dreams or cause us to be defeated by our worst nightmares. Money is perhaps God's grandest experiment. For we have given money such power that it permeates every part of our existence. It is more than a means of exchange; it has become our "other" life. And all too often, it is the life we pay the greatest attention and tribute to, at the expense of experiencing the richness that lies within our unexplored potential.

Our unconscious and unhealthy relationships with money have caused many of our personal and societal problems. One of the ways to explore how these unconscious relationships manifest in your own life is to identify and understand *money types*. Money types are based on "archetypal" patterns, consisting of unconscious habits, thoughts, or beliefs, that are active in every person's life. This book will help you discover how your money types influence your relationship with money.

Learning to identify and work with your money types is a magical and revealing process. It is the key to transforming your relationship with money and your self. As we become increasingly conscious, we often move from one archetypal phase to another. This movement is a necessary part of a journey that ultimately, in our most conscious phase, leads to the enlightened experience of the money Magician and the understanding that by honoring the self, we honor the Spirit. As a reward for our courage in undertaking this journey, we are transformed by our knowledge and realize our power to manifest our innermost hopes and dreams.

Why I Wrote This Book

The purpose of this book is to help you explore the great mystery of money and find your own path to a new relationship with it. This journey is about truth, self-discovery, and enlightenment. It will challenge your belief system about money. It will build the bridge between the past and the present so that you can master your future. It will shake you from the deep sleep of unconsciousness. You will awaken to see yourself for the first time, as the Magician you were meant to be, who knows not only where the source of money lies, but who holds the key to unlocking its magic.

I wrote this book to help you find the key to who you really are and what you are truly seeking. There are as many paths as there are travelers. Yet every path is guided by questions from the Spirit. What led you to pick up this book? What are you seeking? What do you want to change? Let the answers to these questions be your starting point. I highly recommend that you keep a money journal to record your responses to the exercises in the book. Most of my clients have benefited greatly from the insights gained by keeping such a journal. It is also a great way to track your progress as you grow and evolve.

Reading this book is an investment in yourself and your future prosperity. I suggest that you read the book completely and then, afterward, go back and do the exercises in your journal. Resist skipping chapters or reading too quickly. Remember, taking the shortest route often results in unnecessary detours or roadblocks to your success.

Most of all, enjoy the journey! Wherever your destination may lie, use your heart as a guide and Spirit as your compass, and you will surely find your way.

chapter 1

the money game

*Man must choose whether to be rich in things
or in the freedom to use them.*

— Ivan Illich, *Deschooling Society,* 1971

During my seventeen-year career as a financial consultant
and money coach, I have frequently observed the game
people play with money. The primary objective of this game is
to hide the deep layer of anxiety, fear, and shame we feel about
money. Silently, we live with this discomfort, accepting it
as our fate. We become skillful players at this game of hide-
and-seek, but we forget that what we hide still lives within us.
We become disconnected from our inner reality, making it
difficult to understand our relationship with money and its
meaning in our lives. Having relinquished our conscious

awareness of our feelings about money, we have become the pawns in the money game and let money rule our every move.

Unconsciously, we accept that money is our greatest resource, but then we feel we have wasted, neglected, abused, avoided, or coveted it. Secretly, we feel guilty and ashamed and are unable to communicate these feelings to others. How did we, as a civilization, come to not only surrender our power to money but also to deny the control it has over our lives and well-being?

Many civilizations existed before us that never used a currency or even knew what money was. When money finally came into use, it began to shape history and our belief system in profound and lasting ways. Even centuries later, we do not fully understand how money affects our lives or how it shapes our world. Money's meaning continues to elude us. Today, because of the inconceivable power and emphasis we have given it, the money game dictates our daily lives. We make decisions based on our feelings of not having enough money, we change careers because we want more money, and many even marry or divorce because of money. Practically every major decision we make is somehow shaped or influenced by money. Yet rarely do we examine what we're truly seeking. Never before has humankind created a game so widely played that has no rule book, guidelines, or training. It is no wonder we hide. We don't even know the rules!

Some Essential Truths about Money

How did money become so powerful when, in fact, it consists of pieces of paper that only have value to the extent that we believe they do? We have not understood that money, quite literally, is worth nothing without our belief in it. We created it. We gave it value. We made it powerful. And then, as the money game grew, these pieces of paper became our greatest resource, a resource so valuable that many people unconsciously worship money above all else. Now, our greatest misfortune is that without money we feel that we are nothing.

Money is both mysterious and elusive. The more we are defined by it, struggle to get it, and greatly need it, the harder it is to obtain. One of the most amazing keys to having more money comes from universal spiritual law — the greatest of these laws being to surrender to what we cannot control.

We cannot and do not control money. Money is a commodity. Its value changes not only in relation to the economy but also in relation to our consciousness. We cannot control money, but by understanding it, we can obtain what we need. Money is not a part of us. We can never truly own it, because it isn't really ours. And to the extent that we maintain the illusion of money as our safety net, we will be prisoners of our own making. Money will own us if we let it.

Defining the Money Game

Our currency states the truth in four simple words printed across each bill: "In God We Trust." It might as well say, "In Money, Our God, We Trust." That would be more honest. That would let us off the hook by stating openly that money is what we truly believe in. Whether or not we are conscious of it, this truth is woven into the fabric of our existence. We have put our faith and trust in money. This is one of the unspoken rules of the money game. Few of us possess the insight to recognize this basic paradox. We have been programmed to believe in the material and the tangible. As a result, no matter how much money we have or how many possessions we accumulate, we do not experience fulfillment, and our endless search for substitutes to fill the void continues.

Looking deeper into the symbolism found on our dollar, we find many other subliminal messages. First, our money is green, a color that symbolizes growth and resources. On the front of the dollar is a picture of our founding father, symbolizing the patriarchal nature associated with money. In our society, money has a distinctly male energy and is equated with winning and success. The largest money game in the world, Wall Street, is still largely controlled by men, with women representing less than 12 percent of stock brokers. (This patriarchy, however, does not extend to having money. While stock markets are dominated by men, over half of this country's wealth belongs to women.)

In today's world, the Wall Street money game stands at the top of the hierarchy and is the game everyone wants to play. However, the deck is loaded and the stakes are high, since we don't have access to the rule book.

Money has even more hidden meanings. When you turn the dollar bill over, you find the two great American seals: the American eagle and the pyramid with its Latin motto. This more obscure seal is quite telling: inside it is a pyramid, consisting of thirteen stones, representing the original thirteen colonies. An "enlightened eye" stands at the top of the pyramid. The words above the all-seeing, all-knowing eye, *annuit cœptis,* are taken from Virgil and mean "He, God has smiled on our endeavor." At the bottom of the pyramid are the words *novus ordo seclorum,* which translate as "the new order of the ages," also adapted from Virgil. For a country founded on the principle of separation of church and state, there certainly are plenty of references to God on our money!

All evidence suggests that money, God, and religion were intertwined from the beginning of civilization. So it is no small wonder that money has become such a powerful force. Beneath all the symbolism is another hidden message that cuts to the core of the money game: If you're good and you play by the rules, we, the gatekeepers, will show you the way to this powerful resource. In fact, the creation of the dollar was the birth of the first pyramid scheme, more popularly referred to as capitalism.

Money Unconsciousness As the Root of Our Pain

Capitalism and its underlying drive toward consumerism greatly influence the financial infrastructure of our lives and how we deal with money. Perhaps our need for money is as much about sustaining our way of life and the survival of capitalism as it is about feeding our own unconscious needs and desires.

Of this I am certain: Money plays far too great a role in our lives for us to remain unconscious of what it means to us as individuals. We must become aware of its impact on our lives and our choices. Continuing to play the money game and denying that we live in the thrall of money only perpetuates our fears and anxieties, chipping away at our souls. As stated by philosopher Jacob Needleman in his book, *Money and the Meaning of Life:* "Money enters so deeply into our personality and into our psychophysical organism that the personal exploration of money is necessary for the discovery of oneself, the discovery of those hidden parts of human nature . . . that need to be in relationship to our consciousness."[1]

Our lack of awareness about our relationship with money is undoubtedly at the root of much of our pain. It often saddens me to witness the shame people experience over money. In conversations with my clients, I have discovered that much of our money shame comes from feeling like we don't handle it well, that we're "bad" with money. Each of us needs to carefully reexamine the path we are taking toward fulfillment. Fulfillment is not about filling your life up with material possessions. I know the thrill of spending money can feel like an adrenalin-pumping, action ride at Disneyland, but when the ride is over, the rush is gone. This is the experience of pleasure, not fulfillment, and it wears off. The quick-fix approach to money will never cure us; it merely masks our deeper desire for meaning.

Searching for Meaning in the Material World

When I was twenty-nine years old, not long after my divorce, I started to experience an unfamiliar restlessness. Although my marriage had failed, I was in a new relationship that was

---

[1] Jacob Needleman, *Money and the Meaning of Life* (New York: Doubleday, 1991), p. 206.

loving and fulfilling. My business was beginning to take off. I was making more money than I'd ever made before. I was the master of my own destiny, and yet I felt oddly detached from my life. I remember saying to myself, Okay, you've done all this, now what?

Then one day, as I was driving to work, I suddenly made a left turn and found myself sitting in the parking lot of a Porsche dealership. I had never even thought of buying a Porsche. Stunned, I sat for a while in my old but perfectly fine Mercedes-Benz, wondering to myself, What in the hell am I doing here? I truly didn't know. Finally a salesman approached my car and asked if he could help me. I looked him directly in the eye and said, "Yes, I came to buy a Porsche, but I have to do it quickly because I've got to get back to my office." He chuckled, but said he'd do his best to accommodate my schedule.

Two hours later, I drove out of that dealership in a brand-new midnight blue 944 Porsche coupe, fully equipped. I couldn't really afford it, but that salesman just happened to be the owner of the dealership. After talking with me, he thought the car was just what I needed. So, he cosigned for it, telling me if I was ever late on one payment he would personally come and take it back.

How to Know What Is Real in Your Life

For a while that car brought me a great deal of pleasure. I felt successful. People thought I was successful. Some even thought I was rich. It was an enlightening experience. I was the same person I always was. All that had happened was that I purchased an expensive sports car, a status symbol (and one usually owned by men), but it changed my life. I was perceived and treated differently, and not always for the better. People were envious, and my car was vandalized several times. One time, someone carved their feelings about my car into its sides with a key. I also began to attract people who were more materialistic than I was comfortable with. The Porsche never really mattered much to me. It was a fun toy, but I didn't really identify with it. Getting the car did not cure my restlessness. It did, however, motivate me to work harder so that I could keep up with the payments.

My experience with that car forced me to look more closely at what I valued. I had everything I had ever wanted. My problem was, I didn't believe that it was real. Subconsciously, I was looking for some external way to make my success more tangible, and I manifested the car as proof. It did not work. It took a good therapist and doing my own spiritual work to finally learn what was real.

What I learned, and what I hope to impart to you, is that only one thing is real: your connection to Spirit, however you define it, and your faith in that Spirit. There is no other security. Without this connection, we will never feel that we are loved enough, that we have enough, that we are enough. Without this faith, we will not know true fulfillment, regardless of how much money we have or how many things we try to fill our lives with.

Understanding the Energy of Money

Do not misunderstand me. I am not saying that money is bad, because it isn't. I happen to like money: I'm just not attached to it. I am conscious of the energy of money and its impact on our lives. Metaphorically, the energy of money is similar to the concept of electricity. While most of us do not understand exactly how electrical energy is created, we know it exists and that it flows magically through invisible currents that shape and surround the universe. However, even though it is always present and available, it only works for each of us personally when we turn on the switch. This single act of consciousness gives us access to this magical energy and this powerful resource in our lives.

Electricity is created by a magnetic field that has both a negative and positive charge, and this same field of energy exists with money. Money shapes and influences the world around us; it is a powerful resource. Money, too, has a magnetic field that responds to our particular "charge" around it and we are granted access to its current and flow through our conscious awareness and actions. Money magic is about teaching yourself how to turn on the switch! When you learn to use the energy of money consciously, you can create miracles in your life. Conversely, if you use the energy of money unconsciously, it can draw things into your life that you could not possibly anticipate or desire.

It took me a long time to reach this understanding. It is no accident that I wrote this book or that I'm a money coach and financial advisor. I have spent a great deal of my life learning about money. I have chased money, made money, married money, loved money, and hated money. I have experienced the thrill of having it all and the agony of losing it. Put simply, playing the money game can be quite costly. It is the ultimate game of "truth or consequences," in which we learn that without the truth, we are left to live

in the shadow of self-deception latent with unknown consequences.

Why We Lose the Money Game

When it comes to money, most people lead imagined as
opposed to real lives. We imagine what our lives will be
when we're "rich." We imagine the great deeds we can do,
the difference we can make. We imagine what we could
have, buy, or become. We measure the possibility of our
greatness according to the amount of wealth bestowed upon
us. We fantasize instead of living and becoming what we
desire. In the process, we have become disconnected from
our innate power to manifest our own reality.

We have given our power away to money. In effect, we
tell ourselves: "I can't do it on my own, it's too hard, I'm too
tired. Here, you do it for me." We assume that if the money
shows up in our lives, we can be and have what we imagine.
If it doesn't, then we cannot. By living this way, we do not
have to be responsible for what happens in our lives. After
all, we were not in charge of our money. The money didn't
show up; therefore, our hopes and dreams were lost in the
shuffle.

At the other end of the money game spectrum is a different kind of player. These players have already "made it"
and are considered "rich" by most standards. It matters not
whether they earned the money, won it, inherited it, or stole
it: the result is the same; they have money. We think that the
end — lots of money — justifies the means. Most of us
believe that having money will buy us freedom and unlimited options. This isn't true. In my experience, people with

money suffer as much as those without; it is just a different kind of suffering, as evidenced by the hordes made rich in the last bull market who flocked to therapists to treat their "sudden wealth syndrome."

Having all the freedom and options in the world can be a terrible burden to even the most well-adjusted person, and this is even more true if you do not understand your relationship with money. Wealth does not suddenly make personal or psychological problems disappear. To the contrary, it often magnifies them. Having that much power can work against you — and the people in your life — if you're not careful how you use it. Unfortunately, since most of us still carry around a fair amount of unresolved emotional baggage, having money only adds to our load. Now, our baggage is heavier, because it has money in it, lots of money.

People with money play the money game in different ways. They don't have to imagine their lives the way others do. Instead, they feel a need to do something with their lives and with all that money. They have to watch over it, invest it wisely, give it away to the "right" causes, decide how to spend it, and use it to accumulate more. This process creates a tremendous cautiousness; you can't be too careful when you have money. You have to have your guard up, because suddenly it's hard to know whom you can trust. Even J. Paul Getty, one of the richest men in the world, once said, "I find having all this money a considerable burden."

People with money often feel guilty and undeserving. Having money frequently causes relationship problems, especially if one person has significantly more money than the other. People with money often have difficulty with trust and intimacy; they are often envied by their closest friends and family members and are pursued by the greed of others. Observing this cautiousness and difficulty with intimacy in my clients and others caused me to conclude that it is impossible to be truly free if you are constantly feeling the need to be guarded and have difficulty knowing whom or what you can trust. Consequently, wealth without consciousness is but another state of poverty. This kind of emotional and spiritual poverty is often overlooked, because it is invisible on the outside. If we could see inside these people, however, we would see as much fear and loneliness as exists in any state of financial poverty, only we seldom empathize with the rich.

A New Way to Win the Money Game

Because of our culture and our personal histories, we have set ourselves up to lose the money game. Fortunately, we can learn to play it differently. This book will offer you some new strategies for success that can lead you to greater abundance *and* a sense of fulfillment — the kind of fulfillment that comes from within. The money coaching processes described in this book will help you discover your own truth about money and its meaning in your life. Part of this process is to look at how we arrived where we are, both personally and historically, and then to explore ways to move beyond this place.

The eight money types, described in chapter 3, can become a guide to discovering the impact of your past money experiences and creating a new relationship with money for the future. You will learn to identify unconscious beliefs and behavior patterns that block your ability to receive all that is available to you. Recognizing your money type is key to understanding the meaning behind what you are hiding and what you are truly seeking.

As you read this book, and work through the exercises, you will begin to peel back the layers of your unconscious. As you become more aware of how you play the money game, you will learn to identify the obstacles in your path and discover ways to make meaningful change. It is only through increasing your awareness that you can change your relationship with money and begin to play the money game differently. It is time to create your own rules based on your own truth. When you do, you will reclaim your power and begin to manifest the world you truly desire.

We need to stop giving away our power and to learn that the source of money, and of all things, exists within each of us. The most effective and powerful way to tap into this source is through our daily connection to Spirit. Throughout this book you will be asked to look inward, to find your own source. You will learn to harness the power within you. In achieving this, you will hold the key to manifesting your own reality — including money.

Exercise

Grand Scale Imagining

This exercise is designed to help you become clear about your real values. It will help you to define what having money really means to you. It will provide a new framework for understanding the relationship between your money and your life. It is important to always remember what it is you are truly seeking. When what you seek is grounded in your own truth, you are infinitely powerful in your ability to transform your reality.

For this exercise, imagine you have just won the lottery. Your entire life, as you have known it, is about to change forever. Complete the following exercise, answering the questions as honestly, and with as much detail, as you can.

I suggest you start a money journal in which you can record your answers for this and the other exercises in this book. The process of recording your responses in a journal will help you track your progress and provide you with valuable insight about yourself.

1. How much is your lottery ticket worth?
2. How does having all that money make you feel?

3. How much money per month do you plan to give yourself to live on?

4. In what ways will the quality of your life be affected?

5. Do you have any fears about how this money might change you or your life?

6. If given a choice, would you prefer that people know or not know of your newly acquired wealth?

7. What are you going to do with the money? Make a specific plan. Write it down step-by-step.

8. What aspects of your plan are essential to your happiness?

Create an intention for your plan by writing those aspects of your plan that you intend to manifest on a separate sheet of paper. Carry this around with you in your purse or wallet. Read it daily. Meditate or pray for guidance in helping you manifest it. Believe in it so that you may become it.

chapter 2

old games

Knowledge of the universal origins builds the bridge between the lost and abandoned world of the past and the still largely inconceivable world of the future. How should we lay hold of the future, how should we assimilate it, unless we are in possession of the human experience which the past has bequeathed us?

— Carl Jung, "The Gifted Child," 1943

Exploring our historical relationship with money, both our societal past over generations and our own personal experience, is essential to understanding and changing our relationship with it. History has played a significant role in forming the unconscious patterns and beliefs that shape our lives. Carl Jung, the founder of analytic psychology, helped us to understand that the entire human experience is stored in the *collective unconscious* and is manifested in our lives through archetypes. Jung believed that archetypes were collectively inherited unconscious patterns of thought, ideas, and images that exist in our individual psyches. These archetypes, and the collective unconscious, affect our actions, motives, and behavior.

Our relationship with money consists of more than just our personal experience; it also includes another layer of reality that predates our individual lives. Although this unconscious reality remains a mystery to most of us, we are nonetheless affected by it. To the extent that you can lift the veil between the collective unconscious and your own conscious reality, you will be able to understand and change your relationship with money and the role it plays in your life. To simplify this concept, imagine that you are a computer with two separate databases. One of these databases was already stored on your hard drive when you were born and represents the collective unconscious. The other database consists of the personal life experiences you have had from birth until this minute; it holds both your conscious and unconscious history.

One of the things that separates us from other living beings and makes us human is our ability to expand our conscious awareness and, through that new awareness, to alter our reality. This chapter will show you how to retrieve the information that has been stored in your unconscious and explore its significance in your life today. In order to change where we are going, we must first understand where we have been. Although we are powerless to rewrite history, we are infinitely powerful, through knowledge and creativity, to reinvent the future.

Money has preoccupied us and influenced our actions for centuries. For more than three thousand years, money has manifested in many forms from seashells, cacao beans, and slabs of stone to various gold and silver coins stamped with images of gods and political leaders. Yet, in spite of its long history and powerful effect on our lives, money remains a subject that is neither taught nor widely understood.

If the purpose of history is to learn from our past mistakes so that we may apply those lessons to our future, it seems rather remarkable that the topic of money has been swept under the proverbial rug. Have we chosen to disregard the history of money because it is far too frightening to look at? Or have our attempts to understand it, let alone explain it, simply failed? Regardless of the reasons for this avoidance, it remains clear that we must develop a basic understanding of our historical experience if we are to shift our individual and collective consciousness about money.

The Abbreviated History of Money

Just as there have been times of great economic prosperity when civilizations grew to unparalleled heights, there have also been periods when money and its use have disappeared completely for hundreds of years. Money has repeatedly disappeared and resurfaced during humankind's ongoing attempt to exert financial control over our destiny and that of the world.

From the beginning of recorded history, human beings exchanged goods and services as a means of survival. Commodities such as food, animals, fur, tobacco, and even people, in the form of slavery, have been exchanged for other goods and services. This barter of one thing for another, however, had a very different energy from the exchange of money for goods. Early commerce created community out of necessity. People had little choice but to become interdependent, relying on one another for basic needs and survival. Money altered this reality and changed human experience in ways that were inconceivable before its invention. As people began to rely on one another less and less, the experience of community diminished — although we still long for it. Once money was in widespread use, the needs and desires of human beings changed dramatically, and they have grown more complex and challenging ever since.

The Birth of Money

Although money in the form of gold and silver ingots (referred to by the ancient Hebrews as shekels) was used as far back as 3,000 B.C.E. in Mesopotamia, precious metals were too scarce for any widespread trade or economy to be possible. The real birth of money came between 560 and 546 B.C.E. when Croesus, the king of Lydia, began making the first standardized gold and silver coins for the purpose of commerce. This new medium of exchange virtually changed the course of human history and gave rise to the first retail marketplace, giving people far greater access to goods and services than they had ever had before. As money, goods, and commerce increased, so did the human desire for more. It is interesting to note that the Lydians invented not only coins but also the game of dice, forging a relationship between money and gambling that lives on today.

Because of his efforts to conquer other kingdoms and widespread conspicuous consumption, the wealth created by Croesus was all but spent in a relatively short period of time. Although Croesus's empire fell, the money legacy he left behind would shape the world in ways that no one could have imagined.

The neighboring Greeks were aware of the Lydians' success with coins and commerce and, coincidentally, had just discovered silver deposits near Athens. Before long, the Greeks began minting silver coins, and Greece became the center of trade for the eastern Mediterranean world. As the trade business grew, it became a tremendous source of wealth.

Money not only changed the way business was conducted in Greece, it also changed Greek society and extended Greece's ties to the outside world. As a result, social relationships that were once based on established connections and mutual survival no longer bound people together. As money changed the relationships between the Greek people and the world around them, it also changed their values and beliefs. As wealth grew, people began to have more leisure time and to pursue new forms of artistic and intellectual endeavors. For the first time, because of the influence of money, creative human potential could be taken to new heights. In ancient Greece, money gave rise to intellectual, artistic, and spiritual transformation.

Money and Greed: Early Warning Signs

News of coin money eventually traveled to Rome. In no time at all, the Romans began minting their own coins and building the first money-centric civilization in the world.

Although the Greeks established the use of money, the Romans created the first global marketplace and the first consumer-oriented society. Quick to discover how money could buy them almost anything, the Romans went on a spending binge that would ultimately destroy them. (The phrase "shop till you drop" was probably first used during this era!) Rather than becoming producers themselves, the Romans relied heavily on the outside world for goods of all kinds. When they ran short of money, they simply financed large armies to plunder riches from other lands. Between their ever-rising military costs and insatiable and extravagant lifestyle, the Romans finally hit bottom by the end of the fourth century C.E. when their empire fell. This great money-centered society managed to survive for nearly a century, only to fall beneath the weight of its own greed. Instead of facing their own responsibility (as is true of all addicts), the Romans blamed money for their demise. The fall of the Roman Empire was followed by the period known as the Dark Ages, and money, the convenient scapegoat, all but disappeared from Western Europe for nearly one thousand years.

Planting the Seeds of Mistrust

By the beginning of the twelfth century C.E., Europeans had developed such a mistrust of money that even the wealthy did not want to associate directly with it. The Crusaders solved this dilemma by creating a sacred military order known as the Knights of the Temple of Solomon in Jerusalem (in 1118 C.E.). The Templars, as they were known, were chaste and spiritually devout; they were also fierce warriors with sworn vows to protect the Holy Land and the riches of the European nobility. The Templars created a powerful international banking institution by providing financial transactions and protection on behalf of the rich for a fee. They were highly revered, and by all accounts the trust they received was truly earned by their commitment and loyalty to their vows.

At this same time, the king of France, Philip IV, was running short on funds. Known as Philip the Fair, the king was ruthless and vain and had an insatiable appetite. He was a tyrant of the worst kind. Knowing that the Templars had possession of the greatest source of wealth, he set his sights on attaining it. Because he knew how beloved the Templars were, he realized he could not wage war against them, so he set out on a path of merciless persecution. By accusing them of sexual perversion, human sacrifice, sodomy, and cannibalism, King Philip convinced his people that the Templars had obtained their wealth by making a pact with the devil. As a consequence, in 1310 C.E., the Templars were publicly tortured into confessions and burned at the stake. In the aftermath, the Christians lost the Holy Land to the Muslims. This story, as well as the story of Sodom and Gomorrah in the Bible, has been interpreted as a sign of God's wrath over the sins of the people.

After the demise of the Templars, the battle between the church and the state of France over who would control the Templars' fortune began in earnest. Within a year, because of the severe financial abuses of Philip IV, the French empire collapsed, and both the pope and King Philip were dead — leaving yet another lasting impression on the collective psyches of humankind.

The First Gold Rush

Shortly after Columbus "discovered" the Americas, the
Spanish and Portuguese kings began to mine the riches of
native Indians throughout North and South America. Their
hungry pursuit of gold and silver brought a great influx of
money from all corners of the world. This pursuit unleashed
a force that could not be contained.

Between 1500 and 1800 C.E., the Spanish and Portuguese
brought literally tons of silver and gold into circulation.
Unfortunately, the Spanish and Portuguese royalty did not
heed the lessons of their European neighbors. They consumed heavily, and they also could not get enough. So much
wealth flooded their economies that a wave of inflation
began that could not be stopped. There was so much gold
and silver that the rich lined everything in it, from their
buildings to their clothing, wearing their wealth as a symbol
of power and status. Although gold and silver continued to
pour in, the kings spent it faster than it could be shipped.
Eventually, they were forced to borrow from other governments, who did not hesitate to charge them a high premium
for their expensive lifestyles. Jack Weatherford best describes
the force of money created during this time in his book *The
History of Money*:

> In conquering America, Spain opened a pipeline
> that pumped a torrent of silver into the world's
> economy, but Spain was helpless to control that
> flow. Neither Chinese emperor nor Ottoman sultan,
> neither the Persian shah nor Russian czar proved any
> more adept at channeling or controlling it than the

Spanish kings. Spain had unleashed a power that raced around the globe and operated with a force of its own, independent of church and state. The wealth of America had run amok, and the world would never again be the same.[1]

The Last Frontier: Money in America

Although paper money was invented by the Chinese as far back as the first century C.E., its widespread use was pioneered in the United States by Benjamin Franklin, who clearly envisioned the role that paper money would play in modern economic life. Franklin was a deeply spiritual man who valued ideas above money and a staunch advocate of hard work and moderate consumption. (If only Ben could see us now!) By the end of the American Revolution, which was largely financed by paper money, the United States was heavily in debt. American currency had become so devalued that it was practically worthless. In 1780, Congress stopped issuing paper currency and people relied on the old standby, coins. The public distrust of paper money became so great that paper currency remained absent for nearly a century.

Eventually paper money was resurrected by the first Legal Tender Act in 1862, which supported the value of currency with a gold reserve, and continued to be backed by the gold standard until 1971. Faced with economic problems and the Vietnam War, President Richard Nixon recognized that he needed more money than could be backed by the government

[1] Jack Weatherford, *The History of Money* (New York: Three Rivers Press, 1997), p. 108.

or its gold reserves. As a result, President Nixon convinced Congress to take the U.S. dollar off the gold standard altogether. Following in the footsteps of previous rulers throughout history, President Nixon was given free rein to borrow billions of dollars to finance the government.

Today the U.S. dollar is a *fiat currency*, which means that it is created and made legal by our government and is not based on or convertible to anything. Although the U.S. government owns over $100 billion in gold reserves, none of these reserves provides any security against the U.S. dollar. The money we use is backed by nothing more than our belief in it and our government's ability to control it. In 1971, since our money was no longer redeemable in gold, new money was printed and the inscription "Payable to the Bearer on Demand" was replaced with the words "In God We Trust."

So it was that the leaders of our country created the first money system based purely on belief rather than on tangible reality. The words "In God We Trust" stand as a lasting testimony to the fact that our leaders had no idea what the consequences of this choice would be. The fate of our world and of money was placed in the hands of God. Whether our leaders knew it or not, this move placed us closer to the truth about money than ever before.

Money and Its Meaning Today

After thousands of years and generations of human experiences, the subject of money and its meaning still remain unconscious mysteries to most of us. It is time for that to change. Historically, when the power of money begins to expand and reshape itself, the existing financial and social infrastructure has always changed. Today technology has created the fastest, most illusive form of money ever known or imagined — a new worldwide digital currency. The gold harvested in the Silicon Valley unleashed yet another powerful influx of money that flooded the world.

Electronic money flows through invisible currents across the globe with the click of a mouse. Never before has so much wealth had the capacity to move so quickly and to change the fate of so many people in a matter of seconds. We have created such a powerful force, and yet we still fail to understand its greater meaning and relationship to our lives. This lack of consciousness has hurt us historically, creating an environment of economic exploitation. But we can change that legacy if we raise our consciousness about money.

The ability to change and manifest your reality moves in direct relationship to your level of consciousness. If you desire your relationship with money to change, you need to be willing to look at your present beliefs and how you acquired them. As your awareness grows, you will realize your own power to manifest whatever you desire. But first you must travel within to uncover the deeper meaning of money and its purpose in your life.

Money represents the duality of our nature as human beings. It is no accident that there are two sides to every coin and dollar bill. One side represents our individual and collective ability to master the material world. The other side represents our ability to master the spiritual dimension or inner world. It is this inner resource that we have yet to tap.

Until we turn the coin over and explore the spiritual dimension of money and the opportunity it presents for enlightenment, money will always be elusive. Seeking to possess it without understanding its true purpose and meaning will only leave us feeling more conflicted and unfulfilled. Until we understand the true meaning of money, we will remain enslaved by it and the material world. The real journey is not about money: It is about you. It is an archeological dig to the center of the truth of who you really are and what your path and purpose are. The closer you get to your personal truth, the closer you are to the source of life, which is limitless and available to us all.

The New Age of Money

Although we have become increasingly clever at manipulating and even creating new forms of money, we still have much to learn. Our collective history may help us understand the unconscious origins of fear and distrust that surround our relationship with money, but it only presents part of the picture. We must also carefully examine and understand our individual histories and personal experiences with money. In the next chapter, you will learn about how the various "money types" relate to money and you will be able to identify and explore your own primary money type. These money types, like archetypes, are based on subconscious patterns that evolved out of your own personal history. Included in your personal history are inherited patterns of thought, ideas, and images that have been passed down through the collective unconscious. By exploring your money type, you can identify the role these unconscious patterns have played in the drama of your life.

We all have a story. Some of us have bigger or "more compelling" stories than others. Some of us are more attached to our stories and are committed to maintaining our part in the script as our legacy. Others feel ashamed or embarrassed by their stories and feel uncomfortable sharing them. Whatever your personal history with money is, your story must be told so that you can witness it objectively and consciously. The following exercise will help you explore and observe your relationship to money in the context of your personal history. In the process, you will discover how your money type has manifested certain beliefs and behavior in your relationship with money.

Exercise

Your Money Biography

Use your money journal to record your answers to the following questions:

Grandpa han

1. What is your earliest memory of money?
2. How old were you at that time?
3. What was the experience like?
4. How did that experience affect you?

Now, using the answers to these questions as the starting point, write your money biography. Include as many details as you can remember about your experience with money throughout your life. Describe each significant money-related memory: what happened, how old you were, how you felt. Who are the key people in your biography, and what messages, patterns, or behaviors related to money did you learn from them?

Once you've finished with your money biography, ask yourself the following questions:

1. What does your personal history reveal about your relationship with money today?
2. What values, beliefs, or judgments about money are related to your personal experience and/or family history?

3. Which of these values, beliefs, or judgments are active in your life today?
4. Are they working for you or against you?
5. Is this the relationship you want to have with money? If not, what type of relationship do you want?

chapter 3

the eight money types

It is our less conscious thoughts and our less conscious actions which mainly mold our lives and the lives of those who spring from us.

— Samuel Butler, *The Way of All Flesh*, 1903

I think it is safe to say that most people harbor unresolved money issues. These unresolved feelings and experiences create patterns of behavior that are often self-limiting and self-defeating. Looking at how these experiences affect your financial decision making can prove to be one of the best steps you can take toward improving your relationship with money. Money Magic can help you explore your true feelings about money by providing a framework for uncovering your unconscious motivations and behaviors related to money.

In my work, I have discovered eight basic archetypes or patterns that describe how people react to and handle money. By understanding your type, you will discover the reasons behind the conflicts or issues you have with money and take your first step toward reaching your personal financial goals. Once you discover your type, you can use the Money Magic processes to transform yourself into a money *Magician,* which is the eighth money type, the one we all want to be.

Many people create extensive financial plans, but continue to make the same mistakes or fail to implement their plan. Those clients who are willing to explore their inner relationship with money are much more likely to reach their financial goals. They have an easier time making financial decisions and are more successful at manifesting money and realizing their dreams. Clearly, there is a direct connection between having a healthier, more conscious relationship with money and creating prosperity.

It takes time and patience to learn to become a money Magician. The first step is to examine why you want to be a money Magician. Over the years, I've observed eight basic ways in which people relate to money. The eight money types are repeated patterns of behavior that reside in the unconscious. By discovering and evaluating your particular money type, you can begin a different kind of financial education, one that is specific to you. Money therapy provides the framework to explore your personal money behavior in the context of your unique background, beliefs, and experience. Doing this work will prepare you to realize your long-term goals.

The Eight Money Types

Most people fall into one or more of the eight money types. Much like Jungian archetypes or the Enneagram, which define different personality types, this system offers a simple way to identify and evaluate your relationship with money. With this understanding, you will learn how to make conscious choices, and, as a result, the money dynamic in your daily life will improve.

In this book I refer to the eight money types as *players* in the money game. Although we may be successful in most areas of our lives, when faced with money decisions, changes, or crises many people revert to an ineffective, emotional approach to making decisions about money. By understanding your unconscious feelings and beliefs about money, you will be more conscious of your habitual money behaviors and better prepared to change them when they occur. Following are descriptions of the eight money types.

The Innocent

The Innocent takes the ostrich approach to money matters. Innocents often live in denial, burying their heads in the sand so they won't have to see what is going on around them. The Innocent is easily overwhelmed by financial information and relies heavily on the advice and opinions of others. Innocents are perhaps the most trusting of all the money types because they do not see people or situations for what they are. They are like children in the sense that they have not yet learned to judge or discern other people's motives or behavior. While this trait can be very endearing, it is also precarious for an adult trying to cope in the real world. We all start out our journey in life as Innocents; however, as we grow and develop, most of us shed the veil of innocence and replace it with our experience in the real world.

The Innocent's goal is safety at all costs. The primary fear is of abandonment. I have encountered far more female Innocents than male, although both exist. The reason that so many women are Innocents is most likely because women are encouraged by our culture to be unassertive and trusting. The Innocent is often romantically paired with Tyrant or Warrior money types, who both thrive on rescuing the Innocent.

Characteristics of the Innocent Type	
Trusting	Financially dependent
Indecisive	Nonconfrontational
Happy-go-lucky (externally)	Feels powerless
Fearful or anxious (internally)	Represses feelings and beliefs
	Seeks security

The Innocent must learn to claim her own power and find safety in the knowledge of her own capabilities. When she experiences her independence, her fear of abandonment dissipates, as does her innocence. In time, she will become fully capable of experiencing her own power. The Innocent is like Dorothy in *The Wizard of Oz*. She must learn that her power lies not with the wizard, but within herself. Once she does, she can find her way anywhere.

The Victim

Victim money types are prone to living in the past and blaming their financial woes on external factors. Passive-aggressive (prone to expressing their feelings in indirect rather direct ways) in nature, Victims often appear to be Innocents, because they seem so powerless and appear to want others to take care of them. However, this appearance is often either a conscious or subconscious ploy to get others to do for them what they refuse to do for themselves. Victims generally have a litany of excuses for why they are not more successful, and the excuses are all based on their historical mythology. That is not to say that bad things haven't actually happened to Victims. More often than not, Victims have been abused, betrayed, or have suffered some great loss. The problem is that they have never processed their pain, and so it has turned on them. Victims are always looking for someone to rescue them, because they believe they have suffered enough. They carry a sense of entitlement: "I paid my dues, look at my battle scars. Where's my reward?"

Characteristics of the Victim Type	
Prone to blaming others	Resentful
Highly emotional (melancholy or angry)	Unforgiving
	Addictive
Lives in the past	Lives out a self-fulfilling prophecy
Financially irresponsible	
Seeks to be rescued	Feels powerless

For the Victim's paradigm to shift, he or she must learn to understand and heal their past wounds. Of all the money types I have worked with, Victims are the most resistant to unlocking the door to their potential. It's as if at some point Victims decide that their history was much more interesting and exciting than any future they might have. As a result, they form a lifetime attachment to living out the drama of their pasts. After all, when you are the star, producer, and director of your own lifelong soap opera, it can become pretty hard to let go of those roles. It feels risky: there might not be a role like it ever again.

The Victim's primary fear is of being betrayed. Ironically, what Victims do not see is that they are most often betrayed by themselves. Spiritual transformation for Victims comes when they are able to see how their past experience can be a powerful tool and catalyst for change. When Victims travel inward and heal the wounds of the past, they are able to move fully into life. Until they do, however, they are not truly living in the present and certainly have little promise of a future. They are simply living off the reruns, which inevitably become monotonous, no matter how good the story was. Moving out of past-based drama is a deeply profound experience for Victims. Because Victims have generally truly suffered, when they become enlightened, they bring forth a great capacity for compassion, love, and understanding — qualities essential in the making of all great money Magicians.

One of the most dramatic transformations I have ever witnessed involved my client Janet, who was a classic Victim. She came to me desiring to "get her financial act together." She was very smart and had a good job, but was constantly getting into financial difficulty. When we talked about her childhood and her family experiences with money, it became clear that she was repeating an old pattern. Her family was lower middle class and had struggled financially her entire life. She felt that their lack of money and inability to support her financially had kept her from becoming what she always dreamt of being: a lawyer. She managed to work her way through college, but, when her father died, she felt she had to work to help her mother, who still had two children at home.

As a result, Janet felt betrayed and let down. She complained about always having to do everything for herself and not being able to rely on anyone. Emotionally, she was very angry at and resentful of the people in her life. Financially, she had gotten herself into heavy debt, had fallen behind on her bills, and was plagued by creditors. She had been married twice, and during both marriages she felt she hadn't really been taken care of. I told her I could help her only if she agreed to go into psychotherapy, because otherwise she would end up right back in the same boat. Tired of her circumstances, she did. A year later, and after a lot of work, Janet's life completely changed. In therapy she learned to address her anger and feelings of betrayal and began to see how those feelings prevented her from taking responsibility for herself. She had been playing the same tape over and over in her mind for so long that it had become her mantra: "If I'd only been born richer, if my parents had helped me more, if the men in my life really loved me. . . . "

With the help of therapy and money counseling, Janet began to integrate and understand how the Victim dynamic manifested itself in her financial life. She learned she was psychologically invested in being financially unsuccessful. Her lack of success was proof of how she had been robbed of opportunities. Her feelings of betrayal were so deep that she wore them like a badge of honor. The state of her financial affairs was a symbol of how everything had been taken from her. As her awareness grew, she began to take responsibility. She realized the young woman who once had big dreams and managed to put herself through college was intelligent, strong, and capable.

Once Victims work through their anger and resentment, they pass into the light and truth of their true selves. They learn we are our spirit, not what happens to us. But first we must see our true self before we can become it. Janet did not become a lawyer, and she realized later that being a lawyer was not her true destiny. She did, however, become a highly compensated personal coach for corporations and individuals, helping them recognize and remove obstacles to their next level of achievement. She serves as a wonderful example of a money Magician who shares what she learned and turned her personal enlightenment into money, the physical manifestation of the spiritual lesson.

The Warrior

The Warrior sets out to conquer the money world and is generally seen as successful in the business and financial worlds. Warriors are adept investors — focused, decisive, and in control. Although Warriors will listen to advisors, they make their own decisions and rely on their own instincts and resources to guide them. The world is filled with Warrior types, from those who enjoy the sport of business and the skillful art of negotiating to those whose single-minded intent is simply to win at any cost.

Characteristics of the Warrior Type	
Powerful	Confident
Driven	Calculating
Loyal	Generous
Competitive	Rescuer
Disciplined	Wise
Goal oriented	Discerning
Financially successful	

Warriors often have difficulty understanding the difference between an adversary and a worthy opponent. A worthy opponent presents an opportunity to put down the sword and embrace one's potential for growth and transformation. A worthy opponent is usually the person with whom you have the greatest conflict. When we are willing to recognize the lesson this person has to teach, even when it is disguised as conflict, their presence is worthy of our attention. When we acknowledge the conflict as an opportunity for growth, our "opponent" has, in fact, served us. The primary fears of the Warrior are dependence and loss of power. The spiritual journey of Warriors, financially speaking, is to understand what they are truly seeking to protect and to establish boundaries around what is most important to them. This means knowing when and why to pick up the sword, and when to put it down. We all need a bit of healthy Warrior inside of us because the Warrior makes things happen. The question is, at what cost? An enlightened Warrior knows the answer.

Throughout a large part of my life, both as a child and an adult, I was ruled by the Warrior. I was well liked because I was fun, loyal, protective, and trustworthy (common traits in young Warriors). However, I was a fighter and responded fiercely to any act of injustice imposed on myself or others, a trait that created a lot of conflict in my life. I remember my sister asking me, "Why do you always fight back? If you'd just shut up, you wouldn't get into so much trouble." But I was a leader, and I wanted to be in control. Over time my behavior proved to be isolating, because as I matured I recognized that I intimidated people, even adults. Most people would rather not do verbal battle with a Warrior. They tend to be razor sharp, quick, and to know all your weak points.

In doing my own spiritual work, I began to realize that I was pretty heavily armored emotionally and that I was the person whom I most sought to protect. Financially, I was always fighting an uphill battle and could never ask for help. Warriors don't ask for help because they fear that would mean they are weak or in need. By my mid-twenties, I realized I was having a spiritual crisis. An avid reader, I always sought solace in a good book and found it in Shatki Gawain's book *Living in the Light,* which opened my eyes and led me to seek the help of a psychologist. I understood there were parts of myself that I did not see clearly. In my first session, I told my therapist that I knew I needed new skills and understanding before I could move beyond my history and alter the path of my future. Together we embarked on a journey of discovery that changed my life forever.

Not only did I learn to put down my sword, but I learned why I had carried it so long and so close to my heart. It was both a psychological and spiritual journey. On the other side, there really is a light. It is you, the soul within you, which is how God shines through you.

The Martyr

Martyrs are so busy taking care of others' needs that they often neglect their own. Financially speaking, Martyrs generally do more for others than they do for themselves. They often rescue others (such as a child, spouse, friend, or relative) from some life circumstance or crisis. However, Martyrs' gifts have strings attached and they are repeatedly let down when others fail to meet their expectations. The mark of the Martyr is an unconscious attachment to their own suffering.

Characteristics of the Martyr Type	
Controlling	Critical and judgmental
Manipulative	Perfectionist
Long-suffering	Resentful
Secretive	Passive-aggressive
Caretaker	Compassionate
Self-sacrificing	Wise
Disappointed	

The Martyr moves between two distinctly different energies: one that seeks to be in control and is controlling of others and the other that feels wounded like a very needy child. Martyrs tend to be perfectionists and have high expectations of themselves and of others, which makes them quite capable of realizing their dreams because they put so much energy into being right. Like Victims, Martyrs often live in high drama, experiencing a lot of highs and lows and struggling with their attachment to negative experience. They see the glass as half empty instead of half full. Their focus on the negative often keeps them from realizing the deep wisdom that lies within their experience. Martyrs who are willing to do their own spiritual work to heal their wounds have the capacity to become gifted healers and powerful manifesters — money Magicians. (John's story on page 77 is a good example of a Martyr.)

The Fool

The Fool plays by a different set of rules altogether. A gambler by nature, the Fool is always looking for a windfall of money by taking financial shortcuts. Even though the familiar adage "a fool and his money are soon parted" often comes true, Fools often win because they are willing to throw the dice; they are willing to take chances. The Fool is really a combination of the Innocent and the Warrior. Like the Innocent, the Fool often has impaired judgment and has difficulty seeing the truth about things. An adventurer at heart, the Fool gets caught up in the enthusiasm of the moment, caring little for the details. The primary difference between Fools and Innocents is that Fools are relatively fearless in their endeavors and remain eternal optimists regardless of the circumstances. In this regard, Fools are like Warriors because they seem to always land on their feet and are not easily defeated. The Fool also sets out to conquer the world but is easily distracted and lacks the discipline of the Warrior. The Fool is much more interested in making money as a sport or form of recreation than as a serious endeavor. Fools would happily give the shirt off their backs only to realize later that it was their last one.

The Fool does possess some rather remarkable qualities that, if mastered, make him quite capable of becoming a money Magician. The Fool lives very much in the moment and is quite unattached to future outcome. Most of what a Fool pursues is for the simple pleasure of the pursuit. Most of us could learn from this characteristic of the Fool. However, until the Fool becomes enlightened, he will continue to attract money easily, only to have it quickly slip through his fingers because he is simply not paying attention.

Characteristics of the Fool Type	
Restless	Overly generous
Undisciplined	Happy-go-lucky
Financially irresponsible	Adventurous
Impetuous	Lives for today
Optimistic	

The Creator/Artist

Creator/Artists are on a spiritual or artistic path. They often find living in the material world difficult and frequently have a conflicted love/hate relationship with money. They love money for the freedom it buys them, but have little or no desire to participate in the material world. The Creator/Artist often overly identifies with the interior world and may even despise those who live in the material world. Their negative beliefs about materialism only block them from the very freedom they so desire. Creator/Artists most fear being inauthentic or not being true to themselves.

Since it is almost impossible to attract what we are repelled by, the Creator/Artist is constantly struggling for financial survival. This is not because they lack talent or ambition. Rather, they are stuck in a belief system that sabotages their ability to manifest money. Too many people on the creative/artistic path feel that money is bad or lacking in spirituality. This is only true to the extent that one believes it is true. And to the extent that Creator/Artists maintain this belief system, they are limiting themselves and creating a block to the flow of money.

The Creator/Artists who work to integrate the spiritual with the material world will find a solution to their financial struggles. Since they have spent much of their time and attention on their inner journey and creative potential, Creator/Artists already possess many of the qualities necessary to become money Magicians. This money type most needs to accept the outer world and embrace its many dimensions. To stop suffering from the tension they feel between the spiritual and material worlds, they must learn to embrace both worlds as part of their own duality.

Characteristics of the Creator/Artist Type	
Highly artistic and/or spiritual	Detached
	Nonmaterialistic
Passive	Loner
Internally motivated	Seeker of truth

I have worked extensively with creative people and feel a special affinity with them. While I recognize that it can be difficult to live in a world that does not value spirituality or creativity as much as other values, it simply does not help to resent that reality. Doing so only widens the gap between the spiritual and the material rather than encouraging us to find ways to bridge it. My friends and clients who have managed to straddle both worlds are among the most successful and happiest people I know.

Several years ago I encouraged my client Ray, a Creator/Artist money type, to stop putting price tags on his paintings. I asked him to consider letting people offer to pay what they wanted or could afford to pay. I asked him to consider surrendering to the process, to just do his work and to ask God and the universe to support his efforts and to be specific about what he needed. Intuitively I knew he was too attached to receiving a high amount for his work as proof that he was valued. This attachment was causing a constriction in him that was blocking the flow of money. His work was wonderful, but his self-esteem was low. Although Ray was very evolved spiritually and artistically, he was missing a significant piece of the puzzle. It is no easy task to recognize that our resistance is the gateway to transformation.

Ray did not like my advice. He felt that he had the right to ask a certain price for his paintings, and that was that. I let it go. About a year after our discussion, Ray called to inform me that he was leaving to live in Europe. He said, "I finally took your advice, and I've sold almost everything. I have enough money to go to Europe for a year or two, and when I run out, I'll come back." That was in 1995, and Ray has yet to return. Periodically, I get a postcard and a glimpse of him living the life he always wanted to live, free of any self-imposed restrictions. In helping Ray surrender his attachment to how he manifested money, I was able to witness the magic of money flowing to someone expressing his truth and living in faith.

The Tyrant

Tyrants use money to control people, events, and circumstances. The Tyrant hoards money, using it to manipulate and control others. Although Tyrants may have everything they need or desire, they never feel complete, comfortable, or at peace. The Tyrant's greatest fear is loss of control. Tyrants are often overdeveloped Warriors who have become highly invested in their need for control and dominance. While Warriors are often heroic in their true concern for others' welfare, Tyrants are purely self-interested. This money type wants power and control for their own sake and will forsake other people if necessary to gain more of it.

Throughout history, the Tyrant has emerged as the ruler who dominates and destroys with no sign of remorse. Today, Tyrants can be found among the political leaders, business people, and family figureheads who use whatever means necessary to win. The Tyrant is a master manipulator of both people and money. Perhaps it's because the Tyrant type is presented as the image of financial success in our society that so many of us secretly believe money is bad. Television and the media do their part to further convince us that, although we may think we want more money, we fear losing ourselves and becoming caught up in the greed and power — like the Tyrant. It's enough to make anyone hesitate.

Tyrants, however, are not as rich as they appear. Sure, they have everything money can buy (which often does include beautiful people) and never have to worry about paying the phone bill, but they lack many things that money cannot buy. They are often, in spite of their apparent success, very fearful and rarely feel any sense of fulfillment. The Tyrant suffers from a condition I call "chronic-not-enoughness."

Characteristics of the Tyrant Type	
Controlling	Critical and judgmental
Rigid	Aggressive
Manipulative	Unforgiving
Fearful	Secretive
Oppressive	Highly materialistic
Prone to rage or violence	

The Magician

The Magician is the ideal money type. Using a new and ever-changing set of dynamics both in the material and spirit worlds, Magicians know how to transform and manifest their own financial reality. At our best, when we are willing to claim our own power, we are all Magicians.

The archetype that is active in your life now is a starting point for personal transformation. By understanding your own money mythology and the personal history behind your current money type, you will become conscious of patterns and behaviors that are preventing you from being a money Magician. As this new consciousness grows, you will begin to experience money matters in a new way — the way of the money Magician.

The Magician is fully awake and aware of herself and the

world around her. The Magician is armed with knowledge of the past, has made peace with his personal history, and understands that his power exists in his ability to see and live the truth of who he is. Magicians know their ability to manifest lies with their Higher Power. With faith, love, and patience, the Magician simply waits in certainty with the knowledge that all our needs are met all the time. Magicians embrace the inner life as the place of spiritual wealth and the outer life as the expression of enlightenment in the material world. They are infinitely connected.

Characteristics of the Magician Type	
Spiritual	Powerful
Wise	Optimistic
Conscious	Confident
Vibrant	Compassionate
Trusting	Detached
Generous	Open to flow
Loving	Financially balanced
Fluid	Transforms reality
Lives in the present	Tells the truth

Exercise

Identifying Your Money Archetype

As you read about the eight money types, you probably identified with one — or more — of them. Sometimes you can be more than one type, which indicates that you are moving from one type to another or that you have characteristics from several types. However, one money type is usually dominant.

To identify your primary type, go through the "List of Characteristics" on page 53 and check all the characteristics that apply to you, without thinking about which characteristics relate to which type. Evaluate each characteristic in the context of your reactions to, relationship with, and feelings about money and how money affects the relationships in your life. (For example, you may be a very generous person emotionally, but are known to be tight about money.)

Write down all the characteristics that you selected in your money journal. Use the "Key to the Money Type Exercise" chart on page 54 to assign a money type number to each characteristic on your list.

1 = Innocent
2 = Victim

3 = Warrior
4 = Martyr
5 = Fool
6 = Creator/Artist
7 = Tyrant
8 = Magician

Add up the number of characteristics you have in each money type category. The category with most characteristics is your primary money type. If you have a score of five or greater in any other category, this is an indication that this money type is also active in your life right now.

A score of four or less indicates a passive money type. Passive money types represent hidden aspects of the self and, while not generally active in your daily life, they can be triggered during times of stress or when you feel anxious or fearful about money. Passive money types are inert aspects of the self that can be influenced by external circumstances or events. These passives money "energies" that exist within us tend to keep a low profile and remain largely hidden dimensions of our personality.

List of Characteristics

Anxious
Prone to blaming others
Highly emotional
Lives in past
Financially irresponsible
Seeks to be rescued
Trusting
Feels powerless
Unforgiving
Addictive
Self-sacrificing
Resentful
Passive-aggressive
Compassionate
Wise
Restless
Undisciplined
Fearful
Financially successful
Impetuous
Optimistic
Overly generous
Transforms reality
Lives for today
Lives out a self-fulfilling
    prophecy
Powerful
Driven
Disciplined
Goal oriented
Confident
Loner
Seeker of truth
Tells the truth
Nonmaterialistic

Vibrant
Rescuer
Aggressive
Generous
Loving
Conscious
Open to flow
Manipulative
Happy-go-lucky
Discerning
Controlling
Long-suffering
Caretaker
Financially balanced
Passive
Seeks security
Financially dependent
Represses feelings and beliefs
Nonconfrontational
Artistic
Competitive
Prone to rage or violence
Calculating
Critical and judgmental
Secretive
Adventurous
Lives in present
Internally motivated
Detached
Highly materialistic
Indecisive
Rigid
Loyal
Spiritual
Oppressive

Key to the Money Type Exercise

Anxious	1	Vibrant	8
Prone to blaming others	2	Rescuer	3
Highly emotional	2	Aggressive	7
Lives in past	2	Generous	3, 8
Financially irresponsible	2, 5	Loving	8
Seeks to be rescued	2	Conscious	8
Trusting	1, 8	Open to flow	8
Feels powerless	1, 2	Manipulative	4, 7
Unforgiving	2, 7	Happy-go-lucky	1, 5
Addictive	2	Discerning	3
Self-sacrificing	4	Controlling	4, 7
Resentful	2, 4	Long-suffering	4
Passive-aggressive	4	Caretaker	4
Compassionate	4, 8	Financially balanced	8
Wise	3, 4, 8	Passive	6
Restless	5	Seeks security	1
Undisciplined	5	Financially dependent	1
Fearful	1, 7	Represses feelings and beliefs	1
Financially successful	3	Nonconfrontational	1
Impetuous	5	Artistic	6
Optimistic	5, 8	Competitive	3
Overly generous	5	Prone to rage or violence	7
Transforms reality	8	Calculating	3
Lives for today	5	Critical and judgmental	4, 7
Lives out a self-fulfilling prophecy	2	Secretive	4, 7
Powerful	3, 8	Adventurous	5
Driven	3	Lives in present	8
Disciplined	3	Internally motivated	6
Goal oriented	3	Detached	6, 8
Confident	3, 8	Highly materialistic	7
Loner	6	Indecisive	1
Seeker of truth	6	Rigid	7
Tells the truth	8	Loyal	3
Nonmaterialistic	6	Spiritual	6, 8
		Oppressive	7

Identifying Your Money Shadow

A score of five or greater in any category represents an active money type that is present in your life right now. If you are not consciously aware of these characteristics, that is generally because they embody hidden or repressed aspects of your self that you have not been ready (or willing) to look at. However, since awareness is the beginning of transformation, this is an opportune time to look at and understand your "money shadow." We all possess a shadow side that represents those parts of our self that are hidden, secret, or disowned. These aspects are literally fragmented parts of the self that remain unclaimed and therefore, disconnected, from the whole. We learn at a very early age to "put our best face forward" in order to get our needs met or to avoid rejection. This is costly to the self because it causes us to feel we are not seen, loved, or appreciated for all that we are. We feel that we must, in fact, hide parts of who we are.

With regard to money, this "shadow side" contains a great deal of what is real and true for us around money. For example, a Warrior money type is unlikely to feel safe openly expressing a Victim aspect of his personality because it is in direct opposition to his need to be powerful and in control around money. However, if he scored high (over five) in the Victim type, it indicates the Victim is active in his life. One of the common ways this Victim aspect might reveal

itself is around issues of authority. Because the Warrior has not integrated and accepted his Victim
aspect, he may hold a great deal of resentment toward
those who are in positions of authority or resent being
told what do. When the Warrior learns to accept and
embrace his Victim charateristics, his reaction to
authority will begin to shift and have less "charge" for
him. Shadow aspects are another dimension of the
duality that exists within each of us around money
and how it affects other parts of our lives.

chapter 4

redefining your true net worth

What we must decide is perhaps how we are valuable rather than how valuable we are.

— Edgar Z. Friedenberg, *The Vanishing Adolescent*, 1959

We live in a culture where the terms *net worth* and *self-worth* have become synonymous. Yet they have entirely different meanings. Often, if we look closely enough, a far greater truth lies within words than we had imagined. For example, if we separate and dissect the words *net, worth,* and *self,* an entirely different picture comes into view.

According to *Webster's New Collegiate Dictionary,* the two most common definitions of the word *net* are "anything that catches or traps; ensnares" and "a net amount, profit, price, or result; after all considerations; final." The word

worth means "monetary" or "the value of something measured by its qualities or by the esteem in which it is held."
The word *self* means "one's own person as distinct from all
others."

Upon considering the meaning of these words, we discover that most of us feel "trapped" and "measured" by
money, leaving the self alone and unaccounted for. Since we
often do not feel good about our net worth, we internalize
that feeling by devaluing our self-worth. This is because we
do not properly appreciate ourselves for being intrinsically
valuable in our uniqueness — separate from our net worth.

Over the years I have asked hundreds of people to prepare net-worth statements (showing their financial assets
minus their financial liabilities), and without fail, my clients
find this to be a difficult task. Many clients simply refused
to do it. Others would only do it if I helped them. Those
who willingly completed the task were few and far between.
This resistance was so prevalent that I finally realized it was
not the task but the emotional turmoil it caused that was the
root of the problem.

When it comes to our net worth, most of us feel that we
never quite measure up. Believing that how much we have
accumulated is proof of our value is a painful experience. In
our culture, our wealth is the ultimate measure of who we
are. We have become defined by it. Those who have little net
worth feel a corresponding lack of self-worth. But they are
not alone. Many of my clients who have a high net worth
also experience feelings of low self-esteem. The difference is
that, although they have plenty of money, they often do not
feel worthy of it. They appear to have everything, and yet
they feel they are nothing.

I believe this lack of self-esteem is caused by the profound spiritual bankruptcy that is so prevalent in our culture. By basing our lives on the pursuit of money and material gain, we often neglect the self and its inherent longing for spiritual connection, which is unique to human beings. I do not believe this need is simply evolution at work. Rather, it was intended that we value and nurture our spiritual essence above and beyond all else. Without this connection to the self, our true worth is diminished, and life becomes an endless search for substitutes to fill the spiritual void.

We have become ensnared in the net, caught in the money trap. I believe we will not escape until we value our spiritual being above money and material gain. We need to create a new paradigm for living, one that breaks the patterns of the past.

More Money May Not Be the Right Answer

Most of us live burdened with thoughts of lack and limitation, rarely thinking beyond our historic point of view. Yet we are so much more than simply the sum total of our experiences. Yes, we are greatly influenced by our backgrounds and experiences, but there is a truth in each of us that is deeper than any biography of our lives could ever tell.

Ellen's story is a good example of this point. As a child and young adult, Ellen was poor and lived in constant fear. She came from a violent, dysfunctional family, and survival was an issue for her on many levels. But survive she did. She became successful in almost every way. Money and success flowed into her life in great abundance. She was not, however, a happy person. When Ellen first came to see me, she was severely depressed and in psychotherapy. We talked specifically about her money issues. She told me that she needed money to feel safe but that it caused difficulty in her relationships. Actually, it had destroyed every relationship she had ever had.

Attractive, intelligent, and rich, Ellen easily attracted men. The problem was that, over the years, Ellen had built a fortress around herself, and no one could get in. She was not able to trust anyone enough to be truly intimate. With her psychotherapist's help, she was able to work through her feelings about the abuse she suffered as a child and the pain and anger she felt toward her parents. However, the money issues continued to interfere in her relationships. There was still something she needed to understand in order to find her happiness.

As we looked at Ellen's past, we found the only time she remembered feeling safe was right after her father brought home a paycheck because, when there was money, her family was happy, and the abuse would stop. Although Ellen had forgotten this, this memory was played out in her daily life. Ellen knew she was a workaholic and spent most of her time on the job, but she always said it was because she liked her work. Her workaholism was a major problem in her relationships. The other problem was that, although she had a lot of money, Ellen was frugal beyond belief. She didn't enjoy spending her money, and she wasn't good at sharing it. Ellen was a mixture of the Warrior and Tyrant money types.

As she examined her relationships, Ellen saw how she pushed the men in her life away even though they had truly loved her. Although neither of the men she had married had as much money as she did, they were successful in their own right. That fact was the other missing link. Because Ellen's former husbands weren't as successful as her and money was her safety net, she could not stop working so hard because in her unconscious mind she felt they weren't financially reliable. They might not bring in that paycheck, and then what would happen? Subconsciously she felt betrayed, and so she sabotaged her relationships.

Eventually, Ellen saw that by working so hard to create her safety net of money, she never had time to really look at who she was and what made her happy. She had neglected her self. She always loved art but never considered doing it. She loved children but never had them. There was never time for those things. Then one day she called me and said she needed to see me right away. That afternoon Ellen came in and said, "Well, I did it. I solved my money problems. I gave all my money away."

At first I was disturbed, but as we talked I realized that she had made a good decision. She knew exactly what she was doing. She told me, "Money was my safety net, my protector. But it also kept me from living my life. I had to cut down the net so I could be free." For Ellen, the net also served as a barrier that kept her from knowing herself. Today, Ellen lives on a modest income, paints in her spare time, and works with children. Perhaps most important, she has time to be in touch with her self, with who she really is. She has a real life now and is at peace with her past.

The possibility and potential of each individual is far greater than the sum of his or her past experiences. Ellen had lived most of her life enmeshed in her history. Although she had succeeded financially, she was not experiencing prosperity on a personal, emotional, or spiritual level. We have to move beyond our personal histories to see our true value and worth.

Your Money Is Not Your Life

It is no wonder that we suffer such low self-esteem. Our "balance sheet" (financially speaking), if we're brave enough to examine it, often looks pretty bleak. Meanwhile, we feel continually pressed to answer questions like, "What do you have to show for your life?" "What does your financial picture look like?" "What are you doing to secure your financial future?" These are not questions that most of us really want to address.

I have a friend who is one of the most capable, intelligent people I know. He runs two businesses, is involved in the community, and is well liked by just about everyone. Recently he attended one of my money coaching seminars and told me afterward that he felt deeply ashamed about his finances. When I asked him why, he spilled out a story of how, many years before I knew him, he and his wife had major financial problems and had had to claim bankruptcy. He said, "Every day I think about all the people I never paid back, and every day I worry that it might happen again."

I told him that bankruptcy is a choice that deeply affects a person's self-esteem because, "in the eyes of the world, suddenly you are nothing, you have nothing, you have failed. But that is not the truth about who you are. You are a perfect human being, but that does not mean you don't have problems or won't make mistakes. Bankruptcy is about forgiving debt and letting people start over. But you have to be willing to forgive yourself. You have to be willing to let go and move on." My friend was unable to do so. Instead of starting over, he carried his shame with him, and it became a far greater burden than any debt he'd ever owed. I offered to help my friend further, but he could not face the depth of his shame. His net worth and self-worth had both become bankrupt because he could not see his true value, the value of his self.

Money Therapy Life Inventory

Since dealing with our financial histories and money in general can be so difficult, I developed an "accounting" system that makes the process more positive and pleasant for my clients. I call this system "taking a life inventory," which involves two types of accounting. One inventory is a traditional process involving a financial review of assets and liabilities; the other is an inventory of one's life. I have come to the conclusion that doing an accounting of one and not the other is unkind and unjust to us as human beings — not to mention the fact that I can actually get people to do some financial accounting this way and have fun with it.

Investment professionals are famous for lecturing their clients on the time value of money. This concept basically means that while you have the time, you had better make good use of what money you have (also referred to as the value of compounded dollars). For example, if you are thirty-five years old and want to retire at age sixty-five, you have thirty years to use the money you make today to create income for your retirement tomorrow. If you don't take advantage of the time you have now, you will need to save more money, take greater financial risks, or wait longer to retire.

While this is a very valid financial concept, and entirely worth consideration from a logical financial standpoint, it is not the only perspective. The other truth we need to consider above and beyond our financial net worth is what I call the "time value of life." Unlike money, which we can always find ways to earn, our life bank only has so many hours in it — and we don't know just how many hours we have left. Consequently, we need to consider the value of our time and how well we are spending it before anything else, including money, can have any meaning at all. If all we do is focus on money — making it, spending it, or saving it for the future — we take the very real risk of running out of time. Without this understanding, we will always live in a state of spiritual poverty that no amount of money can save us from.

Perhaps if we had a currency with denominations of time printed on it that we actually had to physically spend as we use time, we might value our life hours as we value money. This would at least make us more conscious of how many life hours we spend for every purchase we make and compel us to ask ourselves some crucial questions, such as "How many life hours am I going to have to spend paying for this? Do I really want or need it that much? How much of my life is being consumed by my lifestyle?" Or more importantly, "Is my lifestyle robbing me of my life?" These are questions we need to answer in order to understand our true worth.

Exercise

Your True Net Worth

To determine your true net worth, first you need to conduct an inventory of your life. In your money journal, answer the following questions:

1. How old are you?
2. How many life hours have you spent? (Formula: Twenty-four hours a day times 365 days a year times the number of years/days you have lived. For example, on your fortieth birthday you will have spent 350,400 life hours.)
3. How have you spent your time?

Now do an accounting of how you have "spent" your life. Account for everything that is meaningful to you. Consider this an accounting of your "living" assets, the things that make you feel good about who you are rather than what you have. When you are done, write a list of all the things you still need to do that would fulfill you as a human being. Finally, how many life hours a day are you spending toward meeting these personal goals? If you feel brave, go ahead and do a financial net-worth statement too. It's not only a good exercise, but it will give you some useful perspective on how you've used your time versus your money.

If you can't quite muster the courage to do an actual financial statement, at the very least ask yourself the following questions:

1. How many hours a day do you work?
2. How much money do you make per day (average)?
3. How much money do you need to live on per month?
4. How many life hours does it take to make your monthly income?
5. How much money have you saved?
6. How much money do you owe?
7. How many life hours will it take you to pay off your debts?
8. How many life hours does that leave you with?
9. Is your lifestyle worth it?

Brenda began the money coaching process as an Innocent and gradually became a Warrior. She is now well on her way to becoming a money Magician. She is a forty-three-year-old entrepreneur, artist, and dancer. This excerpt was taken from her money journal and is followed by her answers to the above questions.

I am at a turning point in my life because I recently made the decision to file for bankruptcy after spending part one of my life on making money…acquiring stuff and looking good. Money, property, and prestige was my banner and looking good was my mantra at all costs...and cost it did. At forty-two, every negative pattern that had been in play since I was fourteen had peaked. I had the clothes, done the travel, owned the business, and funded the relationships all so that you would think I was somebody. The last eight years were the inner work, which brings me to where I am now. I am somebody...And if you can't love me for who I am without the stuff then you're not supposed to be in my life. The decision to file for bankruptcy was the final forgiveness I needed to give myself....I would forgive someone else — how about me? I deserved a second chance, too. Yes, I still love money but I've completely restructured my life. At forty-three, the most important thing to me is love and the relationships in my life. They are the only things that you get to take with you.... The love you gave and the love you received, not the Armani suit you bought. So, for me, I'm spending my life seeking my connection with my God...reaching into my heart to love my nearest and dearest...and to love myself through it all.

Brenda's Life Bank

Forty-three years old
376,680 life hours spent

Her "Life Inventory"

Was a professional dance teacher in New York City,
    five years

Danced professionally on stage

Worked in the fashion business in New York

Traveled to China, Tibet, Hong Kong, Thailand,
    Holland, Germany, France, Italy, England,
    Austria, Brazil, Argentina, and Greece

Went to Paris to dance tango and met new friends

Chased tango from Paris to Argentina to San Fran-
    cisco to Los Angeles

Created a dance event to have salsa and tango played

Produced fashion shows

Shopped the world for clients as an image consult-
    ant for five years

Have been clean and sober for more than eight years

Member of the Agape Church for ten years

Traveled to meet my spiritual teachers

Owned a large salon for five years

Have been a hairdresser for twenty years

Rowed on a crew

Was a body builder for four years

Learned to water ski

Snow skis with abandon

Lost and kept off twenty-two pounds

Created my own art studio

Been a painter for eight years

Have had four solo art shows

Sold almost all my work

Have been on my spiritual path for thirteen years

Have "count-on-able" relationships with my friends

Learned to meditate

Have been a godparent to my niece, Rachel

Became the sister I wanted to be to my brother and
sister

Sang in my seventh- and eighth-grade school play

Learned to speak German and French

Genuinely loved the men in my life and grew with
them

Envisioned winning the green card lottery for a
friend and manifested it

Brenda is a wonderful example of someone who, through her commitment to her spiritual path and practice, discovered her true net worth. I know the journey was not easy for her for I have watched her fall down and pick herself up repeatedly. Yet, she never gives up. She is an Innocent who claimed her power in the kingdom within, a necessary lesson for anyone who seeks to become a money Magician.

chapter 5

building a healthy relationship with money

*Man is a knot, a web, a mesh into which relationships
are tied. Only those relationships matter.*

— Antoine de Saint-Exupéry, *Flight to Arras,* 1942

At the beginning of any new personal relationship,
most mature, healthy adults reflect on their past relationships and the lessons they have learned. We seek to
understand and desire to apply these lessons to our new relationships. Most of us do not wish to make the same mistakes
over and over again. We want to get it right. However, the
success of any future relationship greatly depends on resolving our own issues and clearing the way for the new relationship to evolve.

This is also true of your relationship with money. To
have the relationship with money that you desire, you must

first go through this clearing process. Just as not clearing past emotional issues would probably result in the repeating of old patterns and behaviors in a new personal relationship, not clearing the energy of past financial patterns and old money energy will continue to sabotage your relationship with money. But first, let's work to define your relationship with money.

Defining Your Relationship to Money

In working with my clients and their money issues, I always begin by asking them to describe their relationship to money. Their responses often reveal clues about their money types, which helps me to better understand their money issues. Initially most people do not know how to respond. It is rare that someone spontaneously responds by saying, "Oh, I have a great relationship with money. I understand it, I love having it in my life, and it's not really a concern. I always have enough."

Most people do not think of money as something they have a relationship to. I have a client who always used to say, "I hate dealing with money; why would I want to have a relationship with it?" To which I would reply, "You don't always like your mother either, but you have a relationship with her even if it is not always what you'd like it to be. But she's in your life, and you never give up on her. It's the same with money. Your job is to learn how to make your relationship with money work for you, not against you."

In truth, we have a relationship with anything that we are connected to or dependent on. Based on those parameters, money qualifies as something with which we have a relationship. But, aside from the enormous amount of time we spend thinking about it, worrying about it, and working for it, we give money very little of our attention. We base much of our self-worth on money, and since we tend to undervalue our "self," it makes sense that we have not paid enough attention to our relationship with money.

Every relationship that holds any significant value in our lives is a living energy system that needs attention, understanding, and nurturing. It is precisely our inattention to and lack of understanding about money that causes us to have so much difficulty with and conflict about it. That to which we do not give proper care and attention generally does not respond well in return. If we don't water our plants, they whither and die. If we don't clean and maintain our living space, it becomes chaotic and unhealthy. If we don't care for and nurture our relationships with our friends and family, we risk hurting and losing those we love. If we neglect our work or career, we jeopardize our position and can end up unemployed. We must give focused energy and intention to all dimensions of our lives if we expect them to work.

I think it would be safe to say that, because of our denial of what money means to us, most of us have unconsciously abandoned our relationship with it. I have often seen people retreat into fear or anger at the mere suggestion that perhaps they had problems with money they needed to examine. Everyone feels vulnerable when it comes to money. That we are fearful about it is not too surprising when we consider that we have never been properly educated about money or financial matters. We have no training in the one thing that our culture collectively values the most! No wonder we respond in anger. We have been told we need to go out and earn money, but not been given the tools we need to do so.

Conflict over money is among the leading causes of divorce and suicide. What does that say about us? Money affects every aspect of our lives, and yet we know very little about it. It is time to consciously choose to change this dynamic. A shift in our consciousness will not only help us to build stronger relationships with one another, but it will also be a step toward creating a new financial legacy for our children, one built on knowledge and power instead of fear and dependence. But first we must each identify and redefine our relationship with money and its meaning in our lives. Let us turn to an examination of the true nature of money as part of this process.

The Nature of Money

Money represents a powerful energy force that, like the attraction that exists between people, is drawn to energy that reflects its own nature. To invite the power of abundance and prosperity into your life, you must first make room for it. To do so you must create an energy field in your own life that reflects and attracts the energy of money. To create this energy field, let's begin by clearly describing and understanding the qualities of money. The more clarity you have about all of money's traits, the easier it will be for you to consciously take those same characteristics into your belief system. With this information, you can begin to create the space for money to enter your life. Money will become more accessible as you clear the channel and develop an entry way, one that was always there but was previously blocked by unconscious and unresolved issues. Clearing this path requires that you understand and embrace the nature of money. Below I have listed some words that reflect the essence of money.

Money is:

- Alive
- Fluid
- Energetic
- Creative
- Powerful
- Transformational
- Attached to nothing

Money always initially finds its way into our hands by means of creative intention, which is the process of moving creative thoughts, ideas, and imagination into form and action. We, as human beings, are repeatedly offered the gift of money but all too often we do not heed the lessons of the past and use the creative, positive energy of money in a negative way. Throughout history we have blamed money as the culprit for the ills of the time: war, famine, and economic collapse. Money, however, is never the true cause. Lack of consciousness, greed, and hatred are not caused by money — they are part of our nature as beings of both strength and weakness. Money does not cause these problems — people do.

Money As Creative Flow

Money represents a creative energy that is attracted to the creative flow that is present everywhere. Do not forget these words. For as long as your life reflects the essence of these words, you will always attract money. Fortunes are made and lost daily because people do not understand this basic principle and so defeat themselves.

If the creative, fluid, and energetic nature of money is attracted to like qualities, why does so much of it often seemingly end up in the wrong hands? It is because money, as an energy, does not make moral judgments: it is detached. We usually think of creativity as taking a positive form, but it can also manifest itself in negative forms. Money does not distinguish between the two. It simply follows the creative flow. Ultimately, most negative forms of creative energy are destructive. As we saw in chapter 2, throughout history, whenever money has been used to dominate and destroy or to limit the freedom of others, the flow of money has ceased and the society has collapsed. The same dynamic continues today, for both people and governments throughout the world.

The creative energy of money cannot sustain itself when the host energy field becomes dark and no longer reflects its dynamic nature. From a purely economic perspective, money as currency also responds to outside influences such as the ebb and flow of the economy. For example, the major purpose of the Federal Reserve is to control the flow of money. Too much flow causes inflation, causing money to lose value. Too little flow causes a recession or depression because there is not enough money to meet society's needs. The right flow is created when we maintain a balance between too much or too little; when we are satisfied with "enough." We could all benefit from understanding this basic principle. Perhaps then our personal finances and the global economy would be less volatile and chaotic and become stronger, healthier, and more aligned with the positive creative flow.

Cleaning Your Financial House

When building your new relationship with money, you should do your best to start with a clean slate. To accomplish this, you must clean your financial house and tie up any loose ends. Although this can be a painful process, depending on the degree of financial chaos in your life, it is essential in unblocking the flow of creative energy in your life. This process is also important because it helps you free your mind and heart of any guilt, judgment, or negative feelings associated with both your past and current financial experiences. If you do not find a way to cleanse your mind of negative associations, they will continue to block the flow of creative energy, and affect your future financial life.

John's Story

The first time I met John, he said, "I just want you to know up front that I don't trust anyone when it comes to money." I acknowledged his distrust and asked him to explain why he felt this way. He proceeded to tell me how his former wife had ruined him financially and that his children only called him when they wanted money. He was in business with his father, who had also cheated John out of money. John felt that everyone in his life had betrayed him over money, and he had become so distrustful that protecting himself financially was his only goal in life.

Over the next two hours, John slowly began to express the grief and pain that was at the root of his distrust. At one point he began to cry, saying, "I have given everything to everybody. I have taken care of everyone. Who's ever taken care of me?" Needless to say, John operated from the Martyr money type. What he did not understand is that he used money to control his loved ones under the guise of taking care of them. His disappointment about those he had "sacrificed and helped" caused John to act out various forms of emotional retaliation. John failed to understand how he used money as a measure of his love. Rather than actually being loving and giving of himself, he either rewarded or withheld money from his loved ones as a substitute for the love that he did not know how to give. It was no surprise that money was all he had left. Sadly, his relationship with money (as a form of control) not only masked his real love for others but also prevented him from receiving the love he needed. Deep down, John did not believe he was lovable. He ended up manifesting a self-fulfilling prophecy of financial betrayal as proof that no one really loved him, that it was his money they sought and loved. However, regardless of John's attempts to express love with money, money can never replace a real gift of love that comes from the heart.

Over time John learned to be there emotionally for his children and not simply financially. His past relationship with his children was actually a mirror of his relationship with his own father. John's father had also demonstrated his love and approval with money, providing an example of how an archetypal pattern is passed along from one generation to the next. It is not easy work to change a lifetime behavior pattern, let alone one that has been in the family for a few generations. John had to be willing to look at how his attitudes and feelings shaped his relationships and choose to stop living in the shadow of the past.

Eventually, John was able to rebuild his trust by redefining his relationships with money and the people he cared for, including his father. As he released his feelings of anger and betrayal, he was able to access his grief and experience his real loss, which was not the loss of money, but the loss of love. Money coaching helped John discover that he was not seeking to protect his money; he was seeking to protect his heart.

Working with Your Money Shadow

As we see from John's story, our relationship to money begins in childhood with our parents and family members. As a money coach, I have found that the attitudes about money that we learn as children usually remain unconscious, and manifest as shadow energy in our present-day lives. At some point in our lives, most of us have hoped that we would never become like our parents. However, few of us ever emerge as adults without carrying forward some aspect of our parents that we dislike and, therefore, deny in ourselves. This denial leaves us feeling divided.

Learning to connect with the parts of yourself that you have denied is essential to creating a harmonious relationship with money. It is a process of integration in which we learn to love and embrace all that we are so that we may live in "integrity," which means to combine or coordinate separate parts into a harmonious, interconnected whole. This is our greatest and most challenging work. To the extent that we approach this work with both courage and compassion, for others and ourselves, we are individually and collectively contributing to shifting the money consciousness of humanity.

Exercise

Mother/Father Mirror

Your ability to change and manifest your relationship with money moves in direct relationship to your level of consciousness. If you desire your relationship with money to change, you need to be willing to look at how you acquired your beliefs about money and, as your awareness grows, begin to consciously blaze a path to a new, more positive way of being. But first you must travel within to uncover the deeper meaning that money holds for you in order to see both its shadow and its light.

The Mother/Father Mirror exercise is designed to help you explore the characteristics, energies, and attitudes about money that were, and perhaps still are, present in each of your parents. It is important not to censor this information, but allow yourself to be completely honest about your feelings and experiences. You will receive the best results by completing this exercise in a stream-of-consciousness manner. Begin by closing your eyes and, one at a time, visualizing each of your parents (or guardians, if you were raised by someone other than your parents) beginning with your mother. Once you have formed a clear image of your mother, make a list of words that describe the characteristics, energies, and attitudes that you attribute to her relative to money.

Use descriptive words or phrases. Allow the words that describe your mother to pour out from you without analyzing them, until you feel emptied and have nothing more to add. Now, on a separate piece of paper, repeat this process for your father.

If you had a significant experience and memory related to any other primary relatives, particularly grandparents, complete this same process for each of them as well.

Once you have completed the lists for your parents (and any other significant relatives), create a list that describes how you see your relationship with money. What characteristics, energies, and attitudes about money do you possess?

Compare your list to your parents' lists and determine which parent your money beliefs most closely mirror and in what way. Use different colored highlighters, one color for each parent, relative, or guardian, and highlight each item on your list.

Ask yourself these questions:

- Which parent do I most mirror in my relationship with money?
- Which aspects from each parent show up in my own life?
- Which aspects do I consider positive or negative?
- Which characteristics and attitudes do I openly embrace?
- Which characteristics and attitudes have I denied?
- Why would I deny these aspects of myself?

Any aspects that you have characterized as "negative" are shadow dimensions, and represent disowned aspects of your self around money. These aspects need to be understood, accepted, and forgiven. They will also serve as a baseline for understanding your fears, behaviors, and motivations around money.

As you learn to love and embrace all that you are, you will become more available to realizing your true potential.

Using the insights you gain in the Mother/Father Mirror exercise, you can begin transforming your old money beliefs into a new relationship with money that will lead to greater fulfillment, personally and financially.

Taking Inventory of Your Financial Life

It is almost impossible to change your relationship with money without resolving past emotional issues around money. One way to do this is to take an inventory of your financial life. Begin by writing a list of any unfinished financial issues that you want to resolve. This process may ultimately include confronting people, including those you love. Remember to include items for which you may not be completely responsible, such as a disputed bill that you feel is inaccurate or a tax assessment you disagree with. When you are finished, number these unresolved issues in order of their importance or the pressure they put on you. This is your master list, and you want to keep it for future reference.

Take the top three items from the master list and make a "take action" list. For each of the three items on the take-action list, make a decision to take some positive action toward resolving the item within the next week. Focus on resolution and contact each person, business, or involved party and say, "I'm calling to let you know that my intention is to resolve this issue. This is my situation. How can we work this out?" As you resolve an issue, go back to the master list and continue this process until you find a way to work through your entire master list. Try to resist taking on more tasks than you can handle, because doing so may drain you physically and emotionally. The goal of this exercise is to help you feel good about handling unfinished business, not to make you feel bad.

There's a chance that not every situation will work out exactly as you intended. But having everything perfectly work out is not the ultimate purpose of this exercise. It is more important that you consciously make your intentions known and that you act on those intentions. The mere act of putting your intention to work will create an opening for new energy to be channeled back to you. Your faith and connection to Spirit will help facilitate the rest.

Please note: If you are having great difficulty with this process, it may be a sign that you need outside assistance. Do not hesitate to contact a counselor or seek legal or financial assistance if it will help you get the job done. However you achieve it, the end result will be the same: You will feel lighter, have more energy, and be ready to lay a new foundation for your future relationship with money.

One client of mine, Susan, a classic Innocent money

type who took the ostrich approach to money matters, was so completely overwhelmed by her financial problems she was on the verge of a nervous breakdown by the time she came to me. Consumed by bills and debt, she had stopped opening her mail because she simply could not cope with her circumstances. This, of course, only served to make matters worse, because whether she opened them or not, the bills still existed and grew larger over time. She was paralyzed with fear and guilt.

One piece at a time, we began to sift through her unopened mail only to discover that the amount she really needed to pay every month to honor her obligations was fairly manageable. Her problem was that she felt so guilty about her spending habits and so overwhelmed by the large number of bills that she was unable to respond rationally. She ended up hiring a credit counselor, who negotiated payments with her creditors, and an accountant to file her back taxes. She made one payment every month for two years, and it was over. In the meantime, we continued our money coaching sessions.

In time, she began to unravel her personal history and saw how her spending habits were rooted in her unhappy relationship. She was involved with a man for many years whom she loved deeply but who had always been emotionally unavailable and unwilling to commit. Her overspending grew out of her need to "fill up" the unfulfilled aspects of her relationship. Buying things for herself gave her the feeling of being loved and nurtured. For a time, she felt valued. However, as she received less and less from her relationship, she bought more and more for herself — a dynamic that completely shattered her self-esteem and created a financial crisis. In this circumstance, money became a substitute for the love she was missing and craving. In that way, it also became an addiction. She became a member of Debtors Anonymous, and the benefits of that program helped her immensely.

Susan eventually left her boyfriend, resurrected her life, and started a new career in advertising. She now owns a highly successful advertising company and makes more than $300,000 a year. She cleaned up her financial house, cleared her life of negative emotional energy, and applied her lessons to building the world she wanted to inhabit. Before she redefined her relationship with money, there had been no room in her life for positive experiences. Once she created the space for it, the creative flow of money simply followed her there.

Exercise

Looking for Your Perfect Money Relationship

Using personal relationships as a model, think about what kind of money relationship you are seeking. If you were to place a personals ad in the newspaper seeking a partner, you would want to have a pretty clear idea of what you're looking for. Otherwise, you're unlikely to manifest a person with the qualities you desire. The better you understand what you want, the more likely you are to manifest whatever relationship you desire, whether it be with a person, a job, or money. So be clear about the kind of relationship you desire to have with money. Write a personals ad that addresses your intention. Here's an example: "Spiritual being seeking a relationship with money that is trustworthy, fulfilling, cocreative, prosperous, and knows no limits. I am ready to receive this relationship into my life and to embrace this prosperity with care and attention so that together we may realize our greatest good."

When you have written your ad, tape it to your bathroom mirror. Read this written intention aloud every morning as you prepare for your day. As you finish reading it, repeat the following words: "I am willing to receive this perfect relationship into my life and consider it done, and so it will be."

chapter 6

love and power, fear and control

For one human being to love another: that is perhaps the most difficult of all our tasks, the ultimate, the last test and proof, the work for which all other work is but preparation.

— Rainer Maria Rilke, *Letters to a Young Poet*, 1904

As human beings, we alone have a deep need to control the world around us. Fairly early in life, we learn to fear and mistrust what we cannot predict or control. We are uncomfortable with and wary of contradiction, which is why, I believe, we have such difficulty with money. Money is filled with contradiction. It has a duality that is not unlike our own nature as human beings. It is both spiritual and material, creative and destructive, loving and cruel. It has the capacity to help us fulfill our greatest dreams or be defeated by our worst nightmare.

Embracing Money's Duality

If we are to heal our relationship with money, we must learn to embrace its shadow as well as its light. For money is but a mirror that reflects the energy of its beholder. It is essential that we acknowledge this truth so that we can consciously choose which side of money's reality we want to embrace. We must be willing to accept this duality in order to understand it and become familiar with its many dimensions and inherent contradictions.

Everything in life is a metaphorical puzzle of some sort. What we see and believe is real on the surface quite often masks another hidden reality. As I look out on the horizon, I see acres of flat land stretched out before me. For a moment I can truly understand why people was once believed the world was flat. But the world is not flat, and money, like the world, is multidimensional. Until we alter our perspective, we will continue to live in a one-dimensional self-sabotaging world in which money is represented as either one thing or another, good or evil, black or white. This is not, however, the truth, nor does it serve us to believe it.

Money permeates every part of our existence and affects not only our relationship with our self but also our relationships with others. To a great extent, we unconsciously make decisions about money from a position of love and power or fear and control. Far too often, our money decisions are based on fear because when it comes to money, most of us feel out of control. However, fear-based money decisions are reactions, not choices. These fear-based reactions come from our need to control and are therefore lacking in any real power. When we make conscious choices about money based on loving our self and others, we stand in the power and presence of Spirit and can trust that all our needs will be met.

Changing How We Think about Money

The world is filled with images of people who climbed the ladder of success at the expense of others and were willing to sell their souls for financial gain, power, and control. We are given the message that only the financially strong survive. These images, combined with our collective history, have only served to deepen our mistrust of and disdain for money. Years of personal and societal experience stored in our unconscious prevent us from manifesting our rightful abundance. Our negative and fearful associations with money sabotage our efforts to create the life and financial security we greatly desire. For this state to change, we must create a new belief system filled with positive images and a new language that embodies the power and truth of the reality we wish to manifest.

Just as our thoughts about money are infinitely powerful, our words are even more so. A thought given form by words has creative energy and movement behind it. As it moves from intention to expression to action, it grows infinitely more powerful. If we are to learn to tap into our power to create reality, we must become conscious of the content of our thoughts, words, intentions, and actions.

There are many simple ways to do this. For example, when you are experiencing a shortage of money, don't automatically say, "I'm broke." Instead, try to state your circumstances in a positive manner, such as "I'm having a money recess. That just means I need to play (sing, dance, be creative) more and spend less." When your children ask for something, don't give them the old "money doesn't grow on trees" cliché. Tell them the truth. Tell them that money is an important resource and we need to be careful how we use it. If they cry because you won't buy something, tell them you love them but that we don't show love *only* by buying things. Use the moment to show your children how to be fulfilled from within.

Changing How We Think about Ourselves

When it comes to money, people often display behavior that is contradictory to their nature. This behavior represents unconscious and unresolved issues embodied in our money types. Money can and does bring out the best and worst in us. It is this duality that we must become more conscious of. When we can accept our own duality and contradictions, we can consciously choose where and how we want to live. Both the light and the dark exist within us. To deny this is to deny a part of ourselves. When we bring an unconscious feeling into consciousness, we harness its power to create a reality of our own choosing. However, when we deny that feeling, it has a life of its own, chipping away at us internally like a prisoner trying to escape from his own private hell. We must learn to merge the inner, spiritual world with the outer, material world or risk becoming inmates in a prison of our own making.

Allen's Story

The key to changing our financial reality lies in recognizing the patterns and beliefs of our money types as they are expressed in our everyday lives. It is interesting to witness how an otherwise loving and kind person can take on a quite different persona when it comes to money. Allen's story offers a poignant example of this situation. Allen came to see me at the insistence of his wife, who was upset and frustrated by what she referred to as his "financial stubbornness." Allen was an extremely capable and intelligent man. He had a wife and a son whom he loved very much, and he owned a successful business. Both of his parents had died many years before and he inherited a substantial amount of money. This money could have provided a lot of security and comfort for Allen and his family, but instead it became the source of much family stress, in particular in his relationship with his son, Josh. Although Allen had the financial means, he was adamant about not paying for Josh's college education. It was "his" money, and he did not feel that he should have to pay for his son's education beyond high school.

Allen also had a tremendous resistance to investing and, since receiving his inheritance, he had developed some rather excessive spending habits. By the time I met him, Allen had spent all but $150,000 of his inheritance, which was sitting in a money market account and earning a mere 2 percent in interest. The bulk of his inheritance went to purchasing two pieces of real estate — the home they lived in and his childhood family vacation home on the coast of Maine. Allen had paid cash for both properties. The family had not visited the home in Maine more than a couple of times, nor had they rented it out. The combined value of the two properties was over $600,000. The family had almost no other assets except a small IRA account that Allen had started years ago. On the surface, one might not think that this is such a bad scenario, but there is more here than meets the eye.

When I asked Allen how he felt about investing, he proceeded to tell me that his father was a "gambler" who always played the stock market. Unfortunately, his father "lost the game," and part of the money he had lost had been promised to Allen for his college education. Shortly thereafter, his father died, leaving Allen feeling even more cheated. After his father's death, Allen's mother, who had never managed money before, hired a stockbroker to assist her and, according to Allen, the stockbroker "swindled" his mother out of much of her money. These events had clearly affected Allen, although he showed no visible signs of emotion. When he finished talking, I told him that, considering his history, his resistance to investing was understandable. He response was, "I might not be doing as well as I could, but it's my money, and I'm doing it my way." His words helped me understand why his wife had referred to him as "financially stubborn." At this point, I began to suspect Allen was a money Tyrant.

I proceeded to redirect the conversation to Allen's current financial concerns and priorities. He told me he wanted to retire when he was fifty (he was forty-four at the time) and that, other than putting his son through private school, he didn't really have any other priorities. I asked him about planning for his son's college education, and he said flatly that he would not pay for it. I did not respond to the obvious contradiction that Allen was willing to spend a great deal of money on private high school but stopped short of spending a dime on college. He obviously felt committed to his son's education or he would not have paid for private school. This lack of follow-through was odd, especially since he could easily afford it.

Over the course of our lengthy meeting, it became clear that Allen still harbored anger and resentment toward his father for gambling away his college education. At the end of our meeting, I said, "I'm sorry about your experience with your father, but I must say for someone who didn't go to college, you're a very capable and intelligent man. You should feel good about yourself. You've done very well."

Looking rather stunned, Allen said, "Well, thanks, but I never said I didn't go to college. I graduated from Princeton." In that moment Allen revealed another primary money type and the underlying cause of his money problems. Allen was operating from a combination Victim/Tyrant type. Although he displayed all the main characteristics of the Tyrant, his Victim side also manifested itself in direct proportion to Allen's unwillingness to deal with his true feelings.

Allen was still playing out the emotional energy he had for his father. That his father really was a gambler is also suspect. It appeared that there was still plenty of money left after Allen's father died. However, Allen had to blame the loss of his father on something and, at some point, he made an unconscious agreement with himself that he would never be a "gambler" like his father nor be "taken" like his mother. In spite of reality, Allen still clung to the belief that he had somehow been deprived, and he blamed this deprivation on "money and investing." In this way he was a Victim. Since his father had "gambled" and his mother had been "swindled," money was obviously the culprit.

Of course, Allen had not actually been deprived of anything. He went to one of the most prestigious schools in the country (albeit, paid for mostly on his own behalf), and he had a trust fund. He was happily married and had a wonderful son. But deep inside he was a hurt little boy who felt let down by his father, and rather than face his pain, he projected his pain onto his relationship with money.

The Victim at play in his financial life caused him to remain stuck in the past, where he stubbornly refused to let go of false beliefs — so much so that he had alienated his son, who felt rejected by his father's refusal to assist him with college. Josh had performed very well academically, and his father had always stressed the importance of getting a good education. Without Allen's help, Josh could not afford to attend any of the schools he had been accepted to and would most likely have to go to the nearby community college. This situation was hard to believe, since Allen so clearly loved his son. In addition, Allen refused to acknowledge his wife's concern about his spending and her fear that their money was not properly diversified. In denial of his true feelings, Allen, an otherwise thoughtful and loving man, had turned into a Tyrant.

Over the next few months, Allen became conscious of how he allowed his past experiences to define his dysfunctional belief system about money. Somewhere deep inside, the hurt and betrayal he felt toward his father had been transferred to money, even though the losses he had suffered at the hands of his father were purely emotional and not financial. His parents had both died too soon. But rather than feel his grief, he had let himself become a Victim.

The family money represented all that remained of his parents, and although on the surface he appeared selfish, he really wasn't. He was afraid. The truth was that he didn't trust himself with money, and he didn't want to risk letting down his family, so he bought property and made no other financial plans or promises because of his secret fear that he would fail. Allen's story is a great example of someone who is hiding their inner reality while unconsciously seeking comfort in the material world. It also shows how unresolved financial issues often become manifested in behavior that is contradictory to our true nature.

In order to heal his feelings of betrayal, Allen had to learn the greatest lesson of all — how to forgive. As Allen began to understand and forgive his parents, he opened his heart and chose to love them and be grateful for the opportunities they provided. When he could see the truth about his parents, he was able to integrate it into his life. Allen's real healing came when he decided to set aside funds for his son's college education, an act that showed he had truly forgiven his father and let go of the past.

Over time, I taught him how to be a prudent investor. His overspending ceased as he realized that he could do well with money and was not destined to repeat the past. Allen refinanced their vacation home in Maine and rented it out. The rent covered the mortgage, and he and his wife invested $250,000 of the Maine vacation home's equity in the stock market. Over the last ten years, the money he invested grew to almost $1 million. In that same period, the value of that property only increased by $100,000. Allen's change of heart undoubtedly made him more prosperous. Most important, it also saved Allen's relationship with his son. If Allen had not been willing to work on his money issues, chances are his Tyrant money type would have dominated his life. Instead, he was able to become a money Magician. Fortunately, Allen chose love over fear and in doing so surrendered his need to control. Love is always infinitely more powerful than fear. Healing his relationship with money allowed Allen to pass on a new money legacy to his son, one of a money Magician, based on love and compassion, not fear and control.

Couples and Money

Our unresolved money issues become most magnified in our relationships with our partners. Money and sex are the two most powerful energies that exist between human beings and are at the root of most relationship problems. In fact, it is far easier for most people to discuss sex than it is to discuss money. In both cases I have observed that the problem is one of supply and demand, that is, whenever the supply is low, the demand goes up. People caught in this dynamic usually act out of a feeling of lack and limitation, and their fear leads them to want more control. What they don't know is that when we act from a position of love and power, we become more open and available to truly receiving the abundance of life.

I think it would be safe to say that most of us unconsciously allow our relationship with money to whither because we deny what money means to us. I have seen many clients retreat into fear or anger at the mere suggestion they had issues with money that they needed to look at. Although it is a generalization, I have noticed that women respond to money with fear, and men with anger. No doubt this is a result of considerable social conditioning, since historically women were (and to some extent still are) financially dependent on men and felt powerless over their lives and financial destinies. As I mentioned in chapter 3, "The Eight Money Types," many women are money Innocents. They aren't supposed to know about money because that's the "man's job." Although as women we have certainly made significant headway in the workplace, many of us still feel inadequate and unprepared when it comes to money.

Even today, when two-income families are the norm, some women find themselves in traditional relationships where the husband makes most of the major financial decisions. While gender roles are evolving, change can come slowly in part, I believe, because women are often afraid of asserting their financial needs in their relationships. They often feel vulnerable about their financial security and uncomfortable questioning their spouses' financial decisions. I have seen many otherwise strong women become quite subservient to their husbands when it comes to money. As women, we tend to be the emotional caretakers in our relationship. Since money brings up so many emotional issues, we feel it is better left undisturbed. Although it may seem easier to hand over control of financial matters, remaining ignorant actually puts a burden on the relationship.

I have helped many couples create healthier, more balanced agreements about money. I enjoy this part of my work, because I can clearly see how relieved couples are when they balance the power in their relationship. This balance can only be achieved when both people agree to approach money problems from a position of love and kindness, especially when it comes to their partner's fears and apprehensions. In the course of my work, I have observed three common relationship money patterns.

The Traditional Pattern

The traditional pattern is still by far the most common. This pattern most commonly duplicates our parents' money dynamic (or at least our picture of it). In the traditional pattern, the husband takes the lead in the financial decision making. Although the couple may talk about money and finances, especially any big decisions (like buying a house or a car), the final decision is almost always determined by the man. This pattern is not only common in relationships in which the husband works and the wife stays at home, but it is also prevalent in many two-income households. I have asked many women how they feel about this type of arrangement, and for the most part, although they would like to have equal say, they don't feel knowledgeable enough about money to insist upon it.

The Contemporary Pattern

The contemporary pattern is the second most common pattern. In this type of relationship, the couple makes their financial decisions by joint agreement. This arrangement is more common among higher-income professionals, where both the husband and wife have a higher level of financial awareness and sophistication. This pattern fosters a higher level of communication and feeling of security and trust. That is not to say that people in this type of relationship do not experience difficulties with money. However, since an agreement of inclusion already exists, no one partner has exclusive control over money decisions.

The Financially Autonomous Pattern

The financially autonomous pattern is the least common, but it may be the fastest growing. I have observed this pattern most often in relationships between people who have been previously married or in other long-term relationships, are older, and have considerable financial assets that existed before their current relationship. In these relationships, each member of the couple makes his or her financial decisions separately, and the partners do not combine finances and incomes. No doubt the high rate of divorce and the intricacies of the legal system have made many people cautious about forming financial attachments. I have seen this pattern work both positively and negatively in relationships. Couples who are very clear about their individual financial security handle this type of arrangement quite well. However, not many people, regardless of how much money they have, feel financially secure. And often the person with the least thinks the partner with the most should contribute more to the household. Therefore, issues of trust and intimacy can also be common in financially autonomous relationships.

The following is an example of a couple I worked with in a traditional money relationship.

Stan and Diane's Story

I worked with Stan and Diane as their financial advisor for many years before I began doing money coaching with them. They were great clients to work with because they had such a loving relationship and I admired how well they communicated. Then one day they came to see me, and it was obvious that they were in a lot of conflict about money.

Stan was a prominent doctor, and Diane stayed at home taking care of their three children and managing the household affairs. Stan operated as a Warrior type and was very watchful of their financial well-being. Diane was a classic Innocent type who was financially dependent on her husband. She had let go of her teaching career early in their marriage to care for their children. Although Diane was a vibrant and confident woman, when it came to money she looked up to her husband like a wide-eyed child.

As we began to discuss their situation, Diane began to cry and became almost inconsolable. Stan explained that while trying to refinance their house he discovered that Diane had not been honest with him: She had been spending money and hiding the bills. That was hard enough to deal with, but as it turns out, Diane had also been late paying the hidden bills and had bounced quite a few checks, which had affected their credit and was making it difficult for them to refinance their home.

Stan felt betrayed and angry. Diane felt guilty and humiliated. I explained to them that their problem was not at all uncommon. I asked Stan if we could spend some time hearing from Diane about how this happened, because she was obviously in pain and needed to talk. I said to Diane, "I know you feel bad about what happened, but it's important that you talk about what caused this problem. You must really be afraid or you wouldn't have needed to hide. Do you know what you are afraid of?" Diane began to talk through her tears about how hard it was to live in constant fear of not having enough money. She said, "Stan always works so hard to provide for us, but I feel like we're in over our heads and that we're barely making it. Stan's been giving me the same amount of money every month for years to manage the house and kids, but it just keeps getting more and more expensive. I thought I could juggle it and not tell him I needed more. I don't want to put any more of the burden on him. I think I should get a job to help out, but he doesn't want me to work. So I started using credit cards and hoped I could pay them off a little at a time. But then I got behind and I got scared, and now it's all blown up in my face. I know it was wrong, but I was only trying to make things easier."

At this point, I was confused. I asked Stan if they were having financial difficulties, and he said, "Well, my practice is down a little, but we're okay. We just have to cut back a bit. That's why I was refinancing the house." Clearly Diane's emotional conflict was out of proportion to their external financial reality. They did not lack for money. Stan made a very good living, they owned a beautiful home, and they had a considerable amount of money invested. I asked Diane why she thought they were in financial trouble. In the course of our discussion, the source of their problem was revealed.

Stan had been so afraid that Diane would "mess up" their finances that he gave her a monthly allowance and handled all other money matters himself. Diane's personal history, especially her childhood history, with money was chaotic, and Stan knew that as a result she was fearful about money. Consequently, he seldom discussed money with her — he just handled it. Occasionally, he would comment that his practice was down or that the market was down, just in passing conversation. Diane took what he said to mean that they had financial problems. Since, like a true Warrior, Stan went out of his way to shield his wife from money matters, Diane never knew if they had money or not. Left to her own fear-based devices, she became truly convinced they were in financial jeopardy. She chose not to inform Stan that her "allowance" to cover the household expenses was not enough because she felt he was already working too hard. So she hid her spending and the bills, and the problem grew out of control. Stan was acting more like a parent than a partner. As it turns out, that was exactly how his father had handled money in his family.

By not including Diane in their financial life, Stan not only prevented his wife from growing up financially, he actually added to her fear. I worked with Stan and Diane to establish a healthier system of managing their money based on an understanding of each other's needs and fears. Stan agreed to give Diane a check for their household account that was more than they actually needed. He also agreed to give her a check for her own account, since she was uncomfortable asking for what she needed.

I feel strongly that it is unhealthy if either partner has to ask for money from the other. This type of arrangement is damaging to the individual's self-esteem and to the relationship. In this case, Stan was very open to seeing his part in creating their problems and really wanted to help his wife become as strong in money matters as she was in other areas of her life. Stan really loved Diane, but he secretly withheld money from her out of fear that she would mismanage it. The monthly check he gave her left no room for error, which terrified her. He also withheld information from her, which only gave her the opportunity to form false conclusions that sabotaged them both.

This couple agreed to hire an outside consultant to help them organize and update their financial records, and then maintain the system on a quarterly basis. Having this help brought their anxiety level down considerably. Essentially, they instituted an outside checks-and-balances system so that they could keep negative money energy out of their marriage. Over time, Stan began to act less like the father and more like a partner, and Diane grew more secure about money. Both Stan and Diane needed to bring their relationship with money into consciousness. Eventually, they were able to discard their old patterns and beliefs and replace them with a system that better served them, both as individuals and as a couple.

Stan and Diane forgave each other for the roles they played in creating their money crisis. It was heartwarming to witness Stan drop his anger and approach his wife with compassion and love. He clearly understood why Diane had become so fearful and how his own need for control had contributed to her fear. They had each brought their own money types into the marriage and continued to act them out unconsciously until a crisis had occurred. In this case, the crisis was a blessing in disguise that ultimately led to deeper love and understanding between them.

It is a truly rewarding experience when money coaching works out this way. I have witnessed too many relationships in which couples use money as a form of control. Unfortunately, the need for control is constrictive and undermines the love and trust between people. If we can stand together and face these challenges in our lives with love and compassion, we will develop more powerful bonds and have increasing access to the flow of abundance.

Exercise

Money Coaching for Couples

The following exercise will help you understand how the relationship your parents had with money is reflected in your own life and relationships. In many cases, this exercise has helped my clients discover the source of money types that are rooted in childhood memories and experiences.

Questions to Ask Yourselves Separately

1. How did your parents handle money? Were they open about it or secretive?
2. Did you grow up feeling that money was abundant or scarce?
3. What money type best describes your mother? Your father?
4. Was money a frequent source of conflict between your parents?
5. Did you frequently sense that either of your parents were worried or fearful about money?
6. Do you remember being worried or feeling afraid about money yourself?
7. What words or phrases did your parents or other significant relatives use to describe money?

Once you have both answered these questions, share your responses with each other. Take turns reading your responses out loud. Each partner should pay close attention to the emotional experiences often caused by this exercise. This process can be heart opening and revealing. You may learn something completely new about your partner. He or she may become vulnerable in a way you've never seen. You may witness a lot of residual pain, a sign that your partner needs your love and compassion to help him or her heal. To the extent that you are willing to offer this love, your relationship will grow stronger and more powerful. Any money issues that have arisen in your relationship can be overcome when you stand in the light and power of love.

Questions to Ask As a Couple

Now that you asked yourselves the above questions as individuals and shared your answers with each other, sit down together and answer the following questions as a couple:

1. How do you handle money as a couple?
2. Are you in a traditional, contemporary, or autonomous relationship?
3. Are you satisfied with this pattern?
4. If not, what pattern would you prefer, and why?
5. Is money a frequent source of conflict in your relationship?

6. Do you feel your partner is often worried or fearful about money?

7. What words or phrases do you hear yourself or your partner use about money?

8. Were any of these words or phrases used by your parents or other significant relatives?

9. If you have children, how do you think they would answer these questions about your relationship with money?

10. Pretend you are each other's child. What would you like your child to feel and believe about money? Tell each other. If you have children, tell them.

We must all learn to tell the truth about money, to each other, to our children, and to the world. We need to build a new foundation for money in our lives. We need to provide our children with a healthy level of money awareness as they grow. It is time to bring money out of the closet and into our lives, homes, and hearts in new and empowering ways. It is time to choose love over fear, and to surrender rather than to control. For in choosing the light, we leave little room for the darkness to appear and if it does, we need not be afraid for we possess the power to illuminate it.

chapter 7

the path to fulfillment

Rise up nimbly and go on your strange journey.

— Rumi, *The Real Work*, thirteenth century

Our relationship with money begins when we are children, which is also when we receive our first glimpse of fulfillment reflected in the mirror of the material world. As children, we often make unconscious agreements about money that affect the choices we make about our personal path as adults. By the time most children are in elementary school, they have already begun to identify money as an important source for getting their needs met. Adults perpetuate this belief by providing children with an endless supply of material proof of their love and affection. With each passing birthday and holiday, the bar gets raised a little higher, until it becomes increasingly difficult to meet the expectations we have created in our children. Consequently, they grow up believing that fulfillment equals money and the external, material reality it can buy.

We have so confused money with fulfillment that the very meaning of the word *fulfillment* has been lost. True fulfillment can only be experienced internally. It is not something you can buy or acquire; it is an experience of completion and self-realization. It is more a process than a destination. It is not something anyone can give you; it is something you become.

Losing Our Way

One of the ways we can experience true fulfillment is through a deep knowing in our soul that we are on our path and understand our life's purpose. Unfortunately, we are often so disconnected from our own soul that we have difficulty finding our path, and often stop searching for it. We may even stop believing that we have a soul at all. Few of us received the nurturing needed to recognize what would fulfill us personally or spiritually. This is an unfortunate reality, because we all need guidance and encouragement in developing our self-awareness and acceptance of who we are and the gifts we possess. To know one's uniqueness is a powerful experience, indeed. To not know it leaves a hollow space that too many of us try to fill in other ways.

When we are children, our memory of the Spirit is still fresh. Our connection to God and our soul is so close to the surface we can experience our inner light easily and joyfully. Although small in size, children possess large gifts and unlimited potential. As adults we must encourage children to explore these gifts while their memory of Spirit is strong and before they become self-conscious of their spirituality. Children are nearer to their spiritual self simply because they have occupied their human body for less time than adults, which is undoubtedly why they are notorious for speaking the truth. Children come from truth, and it is their primary reality until we teach them otherwise. To watch a small child at play is to witness a soul expressing itself effortlessly. Then one day, the child loses his or her innocence and imperceptibly the person steps in and overshadows the soul. However, the soul is eternal and will deliver us back to our true self, our true life, and our true path. The soul represents the fulfillment that is revealed when we are living in truth and in accordance with our purpose.

As children, we did not experience ourselves as separate from others; we felt connected to everything around us. For this brief time, we all knew true freedom. This freedom did not require money. As we grew up, we became increasingly self-conscious as our sense of self was defined by the people around us, namely our parents, family, and friends. We were told who we were or were not in relationship to others. We came to see ourselves as "good," "bad," "sweet," or "smart" depending on how those we looked up to perceived us.

As adults, we become unconscious of the powerful effect language has on our psyche and self-esteem and become perpetrators, passing this lack of consciousness on to our children, who are most vulnerable to the psychic wounds inflicted by language. Influenced by our own childhood wounds, it is no small wonder that our soul retreats so easily into the background of our life. As our center of truth, the soul is vulnerable to the untruths we are told and tries to save itself by retreating into a deep, more protected place. This experience marks the beginning of our disconnectedness and explains why so many of us have difficulty finding our way.

By the time we reach adulthood, many of us lose access to the truth that lies inside our retreated soul and become simply who we are expected to be. We make decisions about career, marriage, and children based largely on unconscious agreements with the people in our lives. As it turns out, living this way works for some people. But many others yearn for something more.

Finding Our Path

Somewhere along the way, the sleeping soul grows restless and longs to finally express the truth of who we really are. It becomes the still, small voice within that says, "Wait a minute, this isn't the life I wanted. This isn't who I really am! How did I get here? How do I get out?" We look around at the world we've created and begin to question our choices — and feel trapped. At a certain point, we realize we've bought a ticket to a life we no longer wish to live, and that there is no refund.

As a Warrior type, I have fought being defined by anyone and have always felt compelled to help others find their paths. From an early age I knew that I had a purpose and destiny. I did not, however, have a clue what it was. I was born with an intuitive gift of seeing the truth in others. In my work, this gift has frequently allowed me to "see" if someone is on his or her true path. Sometimes I can see the obstacle blocking the person from their path. I rarely reveal this information directly to people but work instead to facilitate their own discovery of it.

We are blessed when we are truly seen and appreciated for who we are. We all need people to witness our greater truth until we can see it for ourselves. Finding our path and purpose can be a lifelong journey. Some people are lucky and discover it early in life. However, most of us struggle with this journey and often fall down or get lost along the way. And that's okay. There is no such thing as a mistake when you are truly working toward finding your path. What matters is that you keep making the effort. Our task is to simply keep moving toward the light until we can see. In the thirteenth century, the great Sufi poet and philosopher Rumi wrote:

> There is one thing in this world that you must never forget to do. If you forget everything else and not this, there's nothing to worry about; but if you remember everything else and forget this, then you will have done nothing in your life. It is as if a king has sent you to some country do a task, and you perform a hundred other services, but not the one he sent you to do. So human beings come to this world to do particular work. The work is the purpose, and each is specific to the person.[1]

---

[1] Jalal Al-Din Rumi, *The Illuminated Rumi*. Translated and with commentary by Coleman Barks. (New York: Broadway Books, 1997), p. 24.

Although the truth is eternal, it not easy to find if we are busy looking for something else. If you're trying to find your path, it will be easier to discover if you stop expecting it to be clothed in money. I often ask the people I work with what took them off their path. They usually answer with conviction that "there's no money in it" or that they "cannot afford to make the change." I can only tell you what I know to be true: You cannot afford *not* to make the change. The price for not changing is far higher than you'll ever know. We can only turn away the gift of our divinity so many times before it is no longer offered.

People come to me wanting to make changes in their lives. They feel they are off course and want to seek a new direction but are uncertain about how to go about it. They frequently feel trapped by their choices. More often than not they feel their only ticket to freedom is money. If only they had enough money, they could make that change. Most people believe that money will cure their problems, will buy them out of the life they're living and into the life they desire. Money is the magic wand, the solution to all our problems. Many of us believe it is the answer to the prayers we often forget to pray.

During the course of our lives, as we have become increasingly disconnected from Spirit, we have lost access to our power. We have become blind to the light within us. The more we have placed our trust and faith in the outside world, the darker and more unfamiliar our inner world has grown. Without the unrelenting voice of the soul, which constantly seeks our attention and never stops trying to redirect us back to our path, we would never find our way. We all possess an inner compass: We just have forgotten how to use it. The soul doesn't say, "Follow me, I'll show you the way to the money." It just says, "Follow me, I'll show you the way." Forget about money! It will show up when it is time. Our task is to simply heed the signs and follow the directions provided by the Spirit within.

Abundance and Prosperity

When we are on the right path, we are more likely to experience abundance and prosperity. However, abundance and prosperity are not the same thing and understanding their differences is essential. Abundance is our most natural state. It means having plenty or more than enough. Yet the concept of "enough" creates a dilemma for most of us. Abundance is very subjective, since what one person considers plenty is a mere pittance to someone else. Prosperity, on the other hand, is a little easier to define. To be prosperous means to be successful or fortunate. We have come to believe that being truly prosperous requires having a fortune. As a result, many people live in a state of abundance without knowing it, because they are seeking the "fortune" of prosperity. In my experience, prosperity does not come easily to those who wait for it or seek it out. Prosperity happens while we're busy doing other things. If our actions are connected to our path, then we will experience the success and good fortune of prosperity for we will know the joy that comes from fulfillment. Answering the following questions in your money journal will help you identify and distinguish between prosperity and abundance in your own life.

Do you feel abundance in your life?

If not, what do you feel is missing?

Do you feel you are prosperous?

What does prosperity look like to you?

What makes you feel fulfilled?

What remains unfulfilled within you?

What are you willing to do today to change the unfulfilled areas of your life?

Finding Your Path to Fulfillment

Fear of moving from the known — even if we don't like our present life — into the unknown prevents most of us from realizing the magic and joy of being on our true path. Every day I encounter people who allow fear to keep them from moving forward into the uncertainty of the unknown. We can draw courage from the knowledge that each one of us is already on a path. Not one of us is an accident. Even if we were not all "planned" by our parents, each of us is still a miracle. God doesn't make mistakes. Everyone and everything has a purpose.

We each have a unique gift to give — something that no one else can give. When we discover, or, more accurately, uncover this part of ourselves, we truly begin to shine. I believe that we often get lost while searching for our true gift because of the misguided belief that it must have something to do with our occupation or vocation. We forget that what we do to earn money is not always a reflection of who we are. Those who find a connection between their path and their livelihood are greatly blessed. I wholeheartedly believe that this is a state of grace available to us all. It does not, however, always come easily or in the package you might have anticipated. It often comes with great sacrifice. And sometimes we wait too long to take the journey, only to find that our chance has slipped away.

Another Wake-up Call

Four years ago, my life's path changed dramatically. Just when I thought I was settling into my new life, I got a wake-up call and realized I was not really settled in at all. It came in the form of a phone call informing me that my close friend and kindred spirit, Barbara, had died. Although she had been ill, I was not prepared for her death. I didn't even get to say good-bye to her. Barbara had been the best friend I could ever hope for. Her life touched me deeply, and her death changed my life immeasurably.

Just two years prior to her death, I had told Barbara that her business was killing her and that she needed to change her life. She was beginning to fade, and I saw it. She cried when I told her and said that she felt trapped and afraid. She was paralyzed by financial fear and did not know how she would survive if she gave up her business. I advised her to have faith and trust that everything would work out. All the signs indicated that she was meant to move on. I told her, "God will support your decision to make this change. But you must find the courage and faith to take the first step and let go. Holding on no longer serves you." Together we worked on finding a way to change her life's direction. Eventually she put her business and her home up for sale. Although she was afraid and did not know what her future held, she knew she could not continue her life as it was.

Unfortunately, it took Barbara almost two years to free herself of her financial burdens. Shortly thereafter, she was diagnosed with leukemia. For months before Barbara's death, my own health had not been very good. The long-term effects of stress and fatigue had worn me down. I knew I was fighting a battle I could not win. I was beginning to see the same signs that I had seen in Barbara, reflected in my own life. I had known for a long time that I needed to make a change. I knew I needed to write. I also knew that we only get so many chances to follow our path and do the work we were brought here to do. After her death, I could feel Barbara's spirit: She was my messenger. I knew that I needed to let go of the life I was leading and my business in order to change my life's course. I had put off living the life I really wanted for too long.

One morning I woke up and said to myself, "I'm selling my business and I'm going to write my book. I've been doing my work and helping other people to live their dreams, and now it is time that I do the same for myself." In other words, it was time to walk my talk. It wasn't that I didn't like what I was doing. To the contrary, I enjoyed being a financial consultant, and I was good at it. However, I knew there was a deeper purpose to my work that I had yet to discover. I was waiting until I had more money and more time, until my daughter was older — all excuses that stemmed from a lack of faith. Intuitively, I knew that I was meant to take this leap of faith. I could no longer delay making this choice.

Exactly one month later, I sold my business and began writing this book. I surrendered to my faith completely, and my faith was rewarded. In the months that followed, new doors opened, and my life was flooded with miracles. My every prayer was answered. I asked for help and received it beyond my greatest hope. Friends and strangers offered their guidance and support. Before I knew it, I had an agent. All the money I needed to facilitate my decision came to me more easily than ever. In less than one year, I signed my first book contract and began writing my first book, *Start Investing Online Today*. Shortly thereafter, the publisher I had envisioned publishing this book bought it and my second book — and dream — became a reality.

There are no accidents or coincidences. When you are on your true path, the universe conspires and collaborates with you in the most magical way. People have told me many times how my story is the exception and not the rule. I choose to see it differently. I think that miracles are happening all the time, all around us. They are simply waiting for us to become available to them. All we need to do is step into them with faith and surrender.

When you can freely express the gift of who you are, you are in direct connection with Spirit; You have access to your higher self, the part of you that holds the key to manifesting your highest dreams. In this place, the possibilities are truly infinite.

Exercise

Your Life Path

To determine where you are in relationship to your true path, answer the following questions in your money journal:

1. Do you feel you are on the right path?
2. If not, do you think you know what your path is?
3. What gifts or special talents do you have?
4. What brings you joy?
5. What aspect of you brings the most joy to others?
6. Is there something you have always wanted to do?
7. What would that be?
8. Why aren't you doing it?

When you have finished answering these questions, take time to be aware of any emotions you might be feeling. What did the previous exercise bring up for you? What feelings of pain, loss, or grief did you experience? It is important to acknowledge and work through these feelings. Write them down in your journal while they are still fresh in your emotional body. This process will help you release and heal any residual pain and clear the way for abundance and prosperity to come into your life.

chapter 8

the alchemy
of faith

Faith — is the Pierless Bridge
Supporting what We See
Unto the Scene that We do not —

— Emily Dickinson, Poem 915, 1864

In my work, I have learned that the most essential ingredient of financial well-being is faith. Without faith people often lack the confidence and trust necessary to manifest a greater reality. I believe that some people are born into their faith. It arrived with them when they entered this world and is as much a part of them as the beating of their heart. Those born with such faith seldom, if ever, question it. The destiny of many who are born into faith is a calling in the ministry. Others nurture the faith of those around them in less obvious ways. Perhaps they are human angels, the guardians of faith and hope on earth. However, they are a relatively small proportion of the population, and the rest of us are left to define, and redefine, our faith, largely in relationship to our experience.

We often move in and out of our faith as it serves us, or so it often seems. It is easy to have faith when all goes well in our lives. It is an altogether different story when our lives are not moving in the direction we want. Too often it is precisely when we need our faith the most that we abandon it or feel abandoned by it, and lose touch with the Spirit in our daily lives.

It is easy to become disconnected from what we never completely trusted in the first place. In our society, faith has become just another commodity that comes and goes. It seldom lasts, because life is often unfair, painful, and contradictory beyond reason. To be fully alive takes a lot of courage. Some days, just getting out of bed takes more strength than we can muster. To do so every day purely on faith is an act few can commit to unconditionally.

My own journey of faith began as a small child when I experienced a spiritual calling and a need to know who and what God is. First I went searching for God inside religion. Since there was no religion or evidence of God in my own home, I thought maybe God was in someone else's house. I vividly remember going to each of my friends' homes and asking them about their God. I wanted to know what religion they belonged to; I asked to go to church with them; I read their Bibles. I was only seven, and I was on a mission. I longed to find what I knew was missing from my own life.

I went to many fundamentalist Christian, Catholic,

Protestant, Jehovah's Witness, and Latter-Day Saints churches. You name it, I explored it. It was quite an education. I did not, however, find God, nor did I connect with any of these religions. In any case, my mother put an end to my mission when one parent reported that when she had asked me where I came from (which I took to mean in the "original" sense) I told her that I was born in a pineapple in Hawaii. Still in the throes of my own discovery, I had needed to make up an answer, but my mother was not amused. Although my mission was postponed, I secretly probed everywhere, reading everything I could, only to announce rather sadly at the age of fourteen that there was no God. It took many years and a great deal of courage to finally find my faith.

The Path of Forgiveness

It was not until I was in my mid-twenties that I began to experience the presence of Spirit in my life. The first specific experience I had was profound. I had gone through a series of betrayals in my life and was feeling alone, angry, and in pain. Nothing in my life seemed to be working. One morning I woke up to the sound of a voice in my room. The voice spoke to me clearly and simply; it said, "It is time to forgive them."

I knew this was the truth. I knew that I could not be free until I could forgive. Those who had betrayed me had proved to be worthy opponents, the kind of adversaries you realize are there to teach you about who you really are. It is truly amazing how a few simple words could change my life forever. Interestingly enough, I did not have to seek out those I needed to forgive. Over the next few months, I was unexpectedly presented with an opportunity to encounter each of them. And with each encounter, and each act of love and forgiveness, I became more free, and so did they.

Those who had betrayed me needed to receive my forgiveness as much as I needed to forgive them. This experience was quite beautiful and affirming. I felt alive and happy once this task of forgiveness was completed. As I began to open up again, new people and opportunities presented themselves to me.

First, I met a wonderful man who taught me to love again. He saw my ability and encouraged me to apply for a position with the 1984 Olympic Games. I was chosen for the position, and became one of the coordinators of the Olympic Torch Relay, making more money than I had ever made before. It was a once-in-a-lifetime experience that allowed me to travel throughout the United States and become friends with some of the most amazing people I have ever known. It was a time of miracles. I saw all that I received as presents from God, with whom I had successfully completed my first collaboration. It was the first in a lifetime of many such collaborations. I learned that forgiveness opens the door to receiving your divine inheritance. If you are harboring resentment and blame, you have closed the door between you and true prosperity.

Elbert Hubbard wrote: "The ineffable joy of forgiving and being forgiven forms an ecstasy that might well arouse the envy of the gods."[1] He is right. When you forgive, the

---

[1] Elbert Hubbard, *The Notebook of Elbert Hubbard.* (Kila, Mont.: Kessinger Press, 1998).

Spirit within you wakes up and allows you to be free and available to the possibilities waiting for you. In working with my clients, I have found that those who were willing to forgive experience a higher degree of abundance and prosperity. Conversely, those who were unwilling to forgive themselves or others seldom move beyond their archetypal pattern.

One of my clients, Sue, was in a twelve-step program and had been doing her spiritual work for years. She was a kind and generous person, but the Victim type was highly active in her financial life. In spite of all the work she had done, she still clung to her "look what they've done to me" story. In her mind, her money woes were the result of terrible acts of injustice perpetrated by others, and that's where her story ended. She could see no other possibility. I told her that it was up to her to undo the past by forgiving all those she felt had harmed her. However, she could not let go of the hurt and surrender into forgiveness. She did not understand that her unwillingness to forgive only served to hold her hostage to the past. I eventually stopped working with her, because I knew that until she was willing to help herself, I could not help her. It was not until she became homeless and was stripped of almost every material thing that she found the courage to forgive.

Forgiveness is the most important step we can take on the path toward fulfillment. Unhealed wounds, resentment, and blame are obstacles that block the flow of good into our lives. It is not necessary to forgive an unjust act, just the person behind it. The act is over and complete. It cannot be changed. The only thing that can be changed is the energy between you and another human being. Freeing up this energy creates more room for you to manifest your highest good. In your money journal, write down your answers to these questions:

1. Who or what have you yet to forgive?
2. What is stopping you from forgiving?
3. Who does not forgiving hurt most?
4. Who will be served most by your forgiveness?
5. Are you willing to release this painful energy from your life?

The Power of Prayer

Even though I felt a connection to God and knew that Spirit worked through me, it took me years to develop what I now know to be my faith. I fell down a lot along the way. During one very difficult period of my life, I sought comfort in prayer; it was the first time I had prayed since I was a child. Through prayer I managed to find my way out of the darkness. The seeds of faith that were planted during my youth grew quietly within, and the faith that I have cultivated since will sustain me forever. I have learned that prayer is the best way to cultivate faith. Cultivating faith has also become an integral part of money coaching. Where I once felt that Spirit was at work in my life on occasion, I now know that it is always at work.

Prayer is the act of being present with God, however you define God. It is how we actively participate and collaborate with Spirit. We can always rely on Spirit to be there for us unconditionally. We are all God's children, but unlike the parents we were born to, God has no expectations of us. God simply loves us and wants us to follow our hearts and our path and to be happy. When we stand in our own truth, we are one with God. Whatever that truth is, if we can learn to hear its voice and follow it, God is with us, holding our hand. No matter where you are in your life, how large the obstacles, how great the fear or pain, faith and prayer are the easiest way to the other side. Find the Spirit within. It may truly be the road less traveled, so take it. We have traveled the other roads only to end up taking wrong turns, missing signs along the way, or going absolutely nowhere at all. This is the one road we can each travel in our own way and trust that we will never be alone or lost.

Prayer As Spiritual Practice

Prayer is the most powerful spiritual tool available to us, and yet one that too few of us understand or use. Many of my clients have difficulty praying. They are always asking me how to do it. I realized that because of our disconnectedness from Spirit, we have actually become uncomfortable with prayer and God. Many people feel they are unworthy of God's presence and that they lack the proper skills to communicate with Spirit. In truth, we all know on a soul level how to talk to God; we have simply forgotten how. Like any language we cease to actively use, we forget the words. But remembering the language of prayer is simply a matter of practice.

There is no one right way to pray. Prayer is a deeply personal, individual process. It does not matter how you pray, only that you pray and that you do so frequently. You will feel and see a difference in your life in direct proportion to how often you pray. Praying daily is the best way to nourish your soul, your life, and your relationship to Spirit. It is the greatest service one can offer to the self.

Prayer is not about being small or powerless. I often encounter people who have great resistance to prayer, only to discover that this discomfort had very little to do with prayer itself. In many cases, our resistance to prayer stems from how small, helpless, and powerless we felt as children. So many of us were wounded in our primary relationships that we developed great blocks to prevent us from ever being that vulnerable again. Many of us had to work hard to get the love we needed. We never stop needing that love. But we've become quite skilled at hiding that we need it and at sabotaging our ability to receive it. On some subconscious level, resistance to prayer is a fear of vulnerability and of not being loved and accepted by God. We fear that we are not worthy. But we are. We are all loved unconditionally by God. It is perhaps the only really unconditional love there is. We need only open the door of prayer to receive it.

Asking for Guidance

To be in the presence of God is to be both humble and powerful in the light of Spirit. Prayer is not about begging, as many people think, but about gratitude and asking for guidance. A good friend, Michael, came to visit me recently and told me he was terribly frightened and in need of my advice. He did not know any longer what he was going to do with his life. He could not physically handle the work he was trained for, and he felt he had no other skills. I asked him what he thought he needed. He said, "I need cash, I just need cash." I asked him how much cash he thought he needed, how much would be enough to make him feel safe and solve his problems. He paused and said, "Well, I think $100,000 would do the job. But I don't know how to get it."

I then asked him to think about what was missing from his life that he thought having the money would help him change. He said, "Well, I have everything I need, more than enough of some things. Nothing is really missing, except I want to be with my mother. She is old and needs my help. I cannot help her there (she lives in Europe), and I cannot bring her here. I'm trapped."

I told Michael he needed to follow his heart. If he needed to be with his mother, he should go to her. Waiting for the money to show up before he could be comfortable making a decision was not the answer. It never is. My friend had enough money to live in Europe for a while. And who knows what would show up for him once he got there. He began to get angry with me. He wanted me to give him "financial advice." I told him he did not need financial advice. He had enough money. My friend admitted he had everything he needed, although he was not rich by any means. What he lacked was faith. He could not trust that if he followed his heart he would be okay. The only solution to his problem, in his mind, was money.

I asked my friend to consider praying and asking for help and guidance. Perhaps through prayer another solution would become evident. He had nothing to lose. I could not make $100,000 appear for him any more than he could. Even if I could, the money was not what he needed. He needed to cultivate his faith. He needed to connect to Spirit. In doing so, he would not only find the answer, but he would also uncover his ability to act from his heart without worrying about the size of his bank account. He was cut off from his power source, his Spirit, and this state rendered him powerless. He believed, as many of us do, that money would give him the power he needed.

Before Michael left that day he thanked me and told me he knew I was right but that he just couldn't do what I said. If he only knew that by cultivating the power within him through Spirit, he could do anything. If only he knew that the source of all creativity, in which all things are possible and where miracles are born, exists within each of us. If we could all learn how to tap into this source, we could be rich in the best sense of the word.

Reconnecting with Your Spiritual Self

In our materialistic world, we spend much of our energy trying to acquire more than what we have, wishing to be someone else, or wanting to be someplace other than where we are. These desires prevent us from experiencing the gifts that are present within us. I believe that a great part of our growing sense of dissatisfaction and disillusionment stems directly from our disconnection from Spirit. We can heal this dissatisfaction by cultivating our faith and reconnecting to our spiritual selves. To collect the disenfranchised parts of who we are, we must remember the Spirit from which we came. We have been so caught up in the material dimension of life, that we have neglected the other dimensions entirely, including our soul and our greatest resource, God.

We did not just arrive here to work and accumulate possessions. We are spiritual beings born into human bodies, sent here with a path and a purpose. We have simply become so disconnected from the essence of who we are that we can no longer consciously remember or relate to anything that is not visible, that does not exist in the material dimension. That does not mean these spiritual things aren't there. They are. They always were. They will still be there long after we are gone.

The greatest tragedy one could possibly suffer in this life is to have lived and died without knowing the beauty and power of faith. It is faith, this connection to Spirit, that is meant to serve and guide us while we are here. Faith is our greatest gift, and we cannot properly receive it without cultivating our relationship to it. This has been my greatest lesson; the lesson I needed to learn, so that I might share this gift with others. I see money coaching and the lesson of cultivating faith as a road leading to a new way of being and seeing.

To cultivate faith, you must step back and look at what you believe and how that belief was instilled in you. So much of what we believe is nothing more than someone else's beliefs or our reaction to them. We took ownership of these beliefs unconsciously. Therefore, we must look inside the box of our beliefs; pull them out, one by one; and reexamine them. I like to use the visual image of a box, because it allows us to separate our beliefs from who we are. A belief has its own energy, and you can choose to accept or discard it as it serves you. For example, here are a few beliefs that have been passed down through our language:

- Money is the root of all evil. (This is actually a misquote from the Bible, which says, "The love of money is the root of all evil.")

- Money is dirty. (As a result, people with lots of money are filthy rich.)
- Money and greed are married to each other.
- The rich get richer; the poor get poorer.
- You can never be too rich or too thin.
- Only the poor know humility.
- I can't afford it.
- I'm broke.
- What money phrases are you (or members of your family) known for saying?

Exercise

Your Belief Box

Take an inventory of your belief box. Many of my clients make or buy a special box in which they keep the insights gained from this exercise so they can reexamine their beliefs as they change over time.

Begin by asking yourself these questions, and write your answers in your money therapy journal.

1. What do I truly believe about money?
2. How did I develop these beliefs?
3. Which of these beliefs do I consciously practice?
4. Does what I practice "mirror" my beliefs about money?
5. Which of these beliefs no longer serve me? (Write them down on another sheet of paper.)
6. Am I willing to let go of what no longer serves me?
7. If your answer is yes, tear up the list from question five. Consciously release these beliefs. You have no ownership of them. They are no longer a part of your conscious reality. It is your choice.
8. Now you are free to choose new beliefs. What beliefs from questions one and three do you wish to continue to choose? What new beliefs do you desire to bring into your life? Write them down.

Put the list from question eight in the belief box. Whether you keep your belief list in a tangible box, your money therapy journal, or your memory, it is important to periodically reexamine its contents and repeat the above exercise, discarding what no longer serves you and adding new beliefs that do. Remember, spiritual practice is a journey requiring commitment of both thought and action. The more you practice, the greater the rewards and the sooner you will become a money Magician.

the magician's guide to money

Every man is the architect of his own fortune.

— Sallust, speech to Caesar, first century

Magicians are masters of the art of transforming reality. To attain this level of mastery, Magicians know they must be fully conscious of their reality and that which they seek to transform. They are students of the past and teachers of the future. However, Magicians seek to live in the present moment in a state of grace and gratitude. They are followers of the light and leaders of the way. They know the source lies within, and they have access to its infinite power.

Magicians are aware of the money game, but they strive not to become entangled in it. They know that the money game is about the illusion that money is the source of security and happiness. Magicians are connected to the real Source, and they believe that money is an unlimited supply of creative expression provided by the Divine Spirit. Whenever money Magicians begin to experience difficulty with money, they seek to resolve the problem within themselves that is creating the circumstance.

The Magician knows that any feeling of constriction about money will block its creative flow. Therefore, a Magician strives to maintain a high level of consciousness and actively seeks to understand and remove any fear or obstacle in their path. Magicians know they must maintain an open and conscious relationship with money. They recognize that money is but one of many resources available to meet their needs. Magicians trust in their ability to manifest the money they need to fulfill their spiritual path and purpose. They know and live the abundant life. The Magician does not seek prosperity for its own sake; rather, she trusts that if prosperity serves her path, it will be received. Whatever the Magician needs in the material world will be provided. The Magician works to manifest what serves his higher purpose and spiritual path.

The Apprentice Magician's Guide

Wherever you are on your path, whatever money types and issues are present in your life, it is essential that you identify and work through them so that you can manifest the relationship with money that you desire. Realize that, while abundance is available and easily accessible to everyone, prosperity, if it does not serve your spiritual path, may not be part of your future. However, you can trust that you will always have enough. When you surrender your money destiny to Spirit, the weight of your financial struggles will be lighter, for you will no longer be carrying it alone.

Becoming a money Magician is a process, a pilgrimage, that consists of the following steps:

1. Understanding how you play the money game and the places where you get caught in the money trap.

2. Taking a close look at your personal and ancestral history with money and understanding how it imposes patterns and beliefs that do not serve.

3. Becoming intimately familiar with the money types that are active in your life. This involves making a commitment to understanding and changing your conscious behavior so that you can create a healthier relationship with money.

4. Becoming conscious of your thoughts, language, and actions in relationship to money. What you think, say, and do have a powerful effect on your ability to transform and manifest your reality. Consciously choose the position of loving kindness so that you can be in alignment with your true power and that of the Source. It is also important that you work quickly to remove feelings of fear and control from your conscious mind.

5. Redefining your true worth and seeing the value of your life in relationship to who you are and the gifts you have to offer. You are infinitely

more valuable than the amount of money you have or do not have. The truth of who you are is not about money.

6. Establishing a new relationship with money based on what you truly need money to provide for you and you want it to manifest.

7. Seeking to know and to follow your spiritual path and purpose. When you do this, you will never be without. Abundance is your divine inheritance. Those who seek the kingdom within will always have access to the outer kingdom and all that it offers.

8. Doing your spiritual work every day of your life. Pray, meditate, connect to Spirit in whatever way works for you and as frequently as you can. You will see your life change in direct proportion to the time and energy you spend paying homage to your soul and connecting with Spirit.

9. Cultivating your faith. Carry it with you always and trust that all your needs will be met. When you can build this trust, you will never feel lost or abandoned.

10. Carrying with you always the powerful elixir of truth and love, the most transformative ingredients in the world.

Magicians are gifted alchemists who practice the art of manifestation through spiritual transformation. The simple formula below is the Magician's guide to prosperity.

The Magician's Formula for Prosperity Consciousness

M = Master of the art of transforming reality

A = Aligned with the universal spiritual principles

G = Guided by insight and revelation

 I = Integrity-based in all actions

C = Connected to the Source

 I = Intuitive

A = Abundant

N = Not attached to outcome

The Magician's Guide to Manifesting Money

Here are nine guidelines for becoming a money Magician. Embrace and integrate each one into your life and you, too, will be able to manifest all that you need.

1. Seek first to build the portfolio of your life. Before you begin to think about manifesting prosperity in your life, you must know your reason for seeking it. What life are you seeking? Begin to build that life day by day, brick by brick. Lay the foundation now for the life you want; do not wait to have money before you begin.

2. Ask yourself what you want money to transform in your life. You must know the answer to this question before you can expect to manifest it. The more specific your answer is, the greater success you will have.

3. Seek the kingdom within first. The secret to

happiness and success should be based on your internal needs and desires. Work to create a life that reflects who you are.

4. Make certain the reality you seek to transform is in alignment with the spiritual truths to which you ascribe.

5. Let yourself be guided by insight and revelation. Develop your intuition about money so that you will know where to focus your intention. Avoid putting time, energy, or money into areas of your life that take you off your path.

6. Resolve to make decisions with integrity and to act with integrity around money. Only you know your own truth: follow that guidance.

7. Ask for what you want and need specifically. Pray for and meditate on receiving all that the Divine Spirit has intended for you.

8. Remain detached from outcome. Trust that you will receive all that serves your highest good and your life purpose. Magicians know that attachment is the root of all unhappiness and disappointment.

9. Nurture your soul and stay connected to Spirit. Stay plugged into this great power Source, and let it guide you on your path.

Charting Your Course

We constantly hear about how important it is to have a good "financial plan" that includes taking a picture of where you are now (your income, assets, and liabilities) and projecting your financial goals into the future.

The results of a financial plan indicate how close you are to meeting your financial goals and offer advice on how to better achieve your desired financial outcome. Financial planning is a very valuable tool, because it not only provides financial perspective, but it also increases your consciousness about the dynamics of money. As a financial advisor, I certainly advocate financial planning. But, unfortunately, financial planners and investment advisors seldom look at the inner life of a person in relationship to creating their financial plan. Traditional planning looks purely at the outer manifestation of people's lives. Even the most sophisticated financial plan in the world will provide little if any assistance unless it mirrors your innermost dreams and desires. A successful financial plan begins on the inside and works its way out into the material world. Money Magicians know that the key to true happiness and success lies in their ability to transform their inner world into a purposeful and prosperous life.

The Pyramid of Financial Planning (Outer Consciousness)

The pyramid of financial planning has been used in the financial world for many years. It has served as a visual aid to help people understand the importance of building a financial future from a strong foundation and then proceeding in a safe, progressive manner. A typical financial planning pyramid appears on page 144.

Traditionally, the key to a successful plan is to start with a strong foundation and move up the pyramid over time. For example, if you were to simply start at the top, with speculative investing (which is what the Fool money type would be most likely to do), you could easily suffer a financial setback that could take years to recover from. However, by adding money to each of the categories over time, you cover all the bases and create a balanced financial life. The goal is to have a balanced portfolio supported by a strong foundation. This prevents an unexpected turn in the market, life event, or crisis from destroying everything you've worked to build.

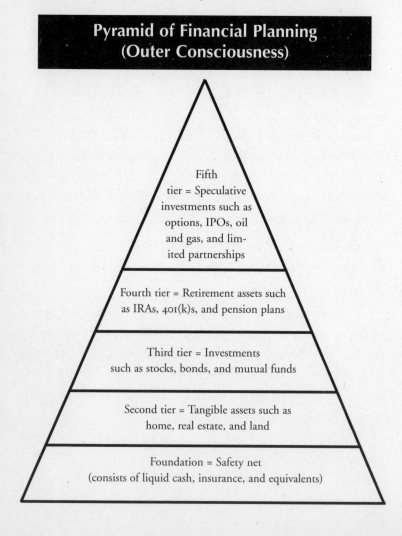

Pyramid of Financial Planning (Outer Consciousness)

Fifth tier = Speculative investments such as options, IPOs, oil and gas, and limited partnerships

Fourth tier = Retirement assets such as IRAs, 401(k)s, and pension plans

Third tier = Investments such as stocks, bonds, and mutual funds

Second tier = Tangible assets such as home, real estate, and land

Foundation = Safety net (consists of liquid cash, insurance, and equivalents)

Building the Pyramid of Your Life

Just as the pyramid of financial planning helps you to achieve your financial goals, your life pyramid helps you establish a foundation for your spiritual goals. This life pyramid helps you stay on track with what really matters to you. It is not up to a financial advisor to tell you what is important to you. This is your life; it's your job to figure out what really matters and how to use your gifts. This part of your plan should serve as a litmus test for determining if what you're creating in the material world is a true reflection of your innermost dreams and desires. It will also help you avoid getting caught in an unnecessary money trap.

A client of mine, Katie, an Innocent who is well on her way to becoming a money Magician, called me recently and said, "I'm thinking of buying a house in Palm Springs. A friend and I were talking, and we think we could afford to buy one if we pooled our money. What do you think of that idea?" My inner voice told me she was moving off focus. She was making great progress, but her tendency to be impulsive was surfacing. I asked her why she wanted to buy a house in Palm Springs. She responded, "Well, I don't think I can ever afford to own a home in Los Angeles, and I've always liked the desert, and it's much more affordable. At least I'll have something when I retire."

I told her that while all her reasons were legitimate, I sensed they were driven by fear and feelings of lack and limitation. She answered, "Well, I guess I need to remove the thoughts about not being able to have what I want here."

I added, "Maybe you need to think about why you

believe you can't have it on your own. Haven't you manifested everything you've needed so far?"

Katie agreed that she had, so I asked her to spend some
time determining if a house in Palm Springs was what she
really needed and whether shifting her focus at this point in
her work would serve her path. Her life as an artist was really
beginning to take off. Diverting time, energy, and money to
allay her fear of not having a place to live in twenty years
might sabotage the reality she was trying to manifest today.
She was still working on her life foundation.

Magicians remain conscious of the motivations behind
their decisions and stay focused on what they really want. A
sudden move in the wrong direction, especially if it is based
on fear, will only be a detour from the real goal. All money
Magicians are very intentional about their choices and how
they use their resources.

The Magician's Prosperity Pyramid
(Inner Consciousness)

Creating a prosperity pyramid will help you clarify your
inner consciousness so that you may rely on it as your guiding strength. Remember, a Magician seeks the kingdom
within as the first step. With this knowledge, you will possess the power to transform the outer world.

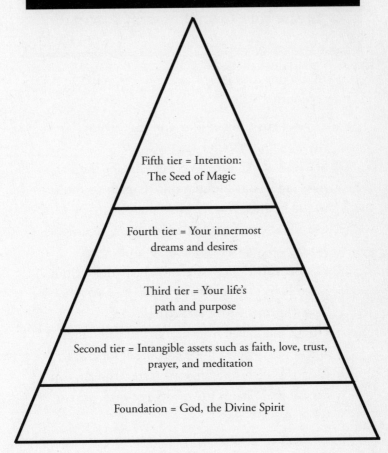

The Magician's Prosperity Pyramid
(Inner Consciousness)

Fifth tier = Intention:
The Seed of Magic

Fourth tier = Your innermost
dreams and desires

Third tier = Your life's
path and purpose

Second tier = Intangible assets such as faith, love, trust,
prayer, and meditation

Foundation = God, the Divine Spirit

Exercise

Create Your Own Prosperity Pyramid

As you do this exercise, record your responses in your money journal.

1. Draw a large pyramid shape and divide it into five equal horizontal sections.
2. Starting at the long bottom edge of the pyramid, label your foundation. Name it according to the Higher Power you believe in.
3. On the second tier, write in all the intangible assets you possess and are committed to.
4. On the third tier, write in your path and purpose. If you do not know what they are, make a commitment to discovering them.
5. On the fourth tier, write in your innermost dreams and desires. These can be tangible or intangible.
6. One the fifth and highest tier, write in your intention. What is the reality you seek to transform in your life?

Now, create your financial pyramid:

1. Draw a large pyramid shape and divide it into five equal horizontal sections.
2. On the long bottom tier, write in the financial foundation you currently have in place.
3. On the second tier, write in the tangible assets you own (type and amount).
4. On the third tier, write in the investments you have (type and amount).

5. On the fourth tier, write in your retirement assets (type and amount).
6. On the fifth tier, write in any speculative investments you have (type and amount).

Based on your financial pyramid, ask yourself:

1. How strong is your foundation?
2. How balanced is your pyramid?
3. What areas need reinforcement?
4. Create a plan that implements the changes necessary to achieve a balanced financial life.

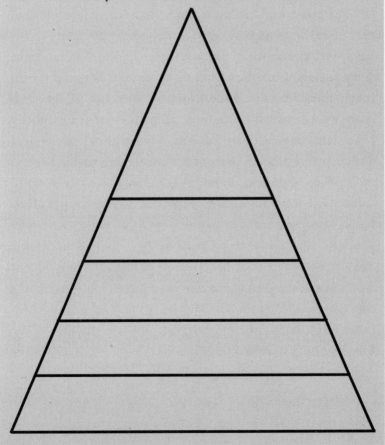

The Pilgrimage of the Magi

The root word for magician is *magi*. One of the earliest uses of the word *magi* is the biblical reference to the three wise men. The magi were guided by the light of a star in the Far East that led them on a pilgrimage to Israel to pay homage to the newborn King, the Son of God. Each one brought a different gift: gold, frankincense, and myrrh. The three wise men were also referred to as kings, because they possessed the knowledge of the kingdom within. They followed the light that led them to the Source and paid homage to the Source with their gifts. Each possessed a different gift and had traveled far to give it. No gift was perceived as more valuable than the others. They were equally valued before God.

This story serves as a wonderful metaphor for would-be money Magicians. We are all on a journey. While the path may not be clearly marked, if we have faith and ask for guidance, we will be shown the way. Like the three magi, money Magicians are guided by the light from within. This light is available to everyone whose eyes are willing to see beyond the visible. Magicians do not wait for money to show up to embark on their pilgrimage. They travel with the gifts they have. They pay homage to the Source by using their gifts wisely. They have faith and trust in their divine inheritance, not knowing when or how it will manifest. They do not worry about the details, for that is not their job. They know they are capable of manifesting whatever they need to help them fulfill their path and purpose. To this end, they know they will be given everything.

For many years, I struggled with why I never seemed to

"get ahead" financially. I always worked very hard and took more risks than most people. It somehow seemed unfair to me that I wasn't more financially successful, given my efforts. Sure, I made a very good living, but I still felt somewhat cheated that I wasn't "rich."

Then one day it hit me that I had not been seeing my life correctly. I always valued my personal freedom and independence above everything, and I knew my home environment was essential to my sense of peace and well-being. As I did an accounting of my life, I saw how everything had worked in the most synchronistic way to create the life that I most valued. I have been self-employed most of my life. I have been completely financially independent since I was seventeen years old. I have traveled extensively. I have lived in some of the most wonderful places on the Earth. Each time I moved, my family and friends came to visit and say, "How do you keep finding these wonderful places?" I answered them with, "I just keep asking for what I need."

I realized I am a money Magician. I know how to create and manifest everything I need, including money, to support my path and the life I have chosen. I have enough of everything. I am as "rich" and prosperous as anyone I know. I realized another important fact: having too much money too soon often takes people off their path. For instance, I know that if I had made a fortune early in my life, I most likely would not have stayed on this path. I would not have endured the hardships or learned the lessons that were necessary to bring me to this point. The consequences of moving off my path would have been immeasurable, for I would not have met the people I have known or had the opportunity to do this work or to help people change their lives. And chances are, I would not have written this book.

When I graduated from college as an English major, I gave up the idea of being a writer and a teacher because I was tired of being poor. I was too familiar with poverty, and I was ready to be prosperous. Well, twenty years have passed and I have come full circle to my original purpose, to serve as a writer, a teacher, and money coach. It was my path all along.

Listen to the Spirit within. You too will be guided to take the path that you were meant to travel. It may not always be easy, but everything will turn out as it should. You will know what it is to live in abundance. You may even experience tremendous prosperity. So let go, and do not be afraid. Risk everything if you have to. Trust that you will be taken care of — and you will be. Whoever and wherever you are right now, take that first step and begin your journey. Everything you need is available to you. If you know the way, follow it. If you don't know the way, seek guidance. Ask and you shall receive.

chapter 10

where do we go from here?

The aim of life is to live, and to live means to be aware,
joyously, drunkenly, serenely, divinely aware.
— Henry Miller, *The Wisdom of the Heart,* 1941

The most important asset you will ever possess is the life you were given. What you choose to do with this gift in the relatively short period of time you have possession of it will determine whether or not you leave this world as wealthy as you came in. For you were given all you ever needed in the seed of possibility that was born as you. You are a miracle. Anyone, including you, who tells you differently is wrong. Remember the truth, and live your life surrounded by this knowledge. Form a circle of belief around yourself that says: "I am a miracle; the seed of infinite possibility was born

within me and is with me still." Do not let anyone or anything that happens to you alter this belief, for it is an eternal
truth.

On the morning I began writing the conclusion to this
book, my inner guide said, "Pay attention to the landscape
of your life." So I wandered outside and was drawn to a
magnificent old tree in my front yard that I often sit with
and observe. This old pine possesses a majesty and wisdom
I have always found comforting. Nature is such a powerful
teacher. As I meditated, I began thinking about how long
ago this tree began its journey from a seed.

The tree must be more than two hundred years old. It
has such a simple life. It does not have to do or think
about anything to be beautiful. It does not have to process
change, for its changes occur naturally. It does not have to
be conscious or make choices. The tree does not have to do
anything. It just is. What began as a seed grew almost effortlessly to tremendous heights. It has expanded in many ways,
in both depth and height and has many branches that
extend and lift up to the sky. It has gone through many sea-
sons and changes during its long life, all because of one tiny
seed that was planted long ago. The tree has a purpose that
it simply lives every day.

God is the most magnificent artist. Every living thing we
see existed first in the imagination of the Divine Spirit.
Everything in nature was beautifully painted and crafted
into form with intention and purpose. Of course, the difference between the tree and us is that we were given the
power of creative thought and free will. These are the gifts
that make us human. We were given life, a blank canvas,
and an imagination of our own to paint and create our own

reality. Unlike the tree, whose entire reality was born of a single seed, we must use the gifts we've been given — creativity, imagination, consciousness, and free will — to grow into the fullness of our being. We must grow the seed of our potential by working the soil of our life daily. When we forget to do this, we are wasting the wealth hidden in our potential.

Think about it. If every day, not just some day (which is an illusion anyway), you planted a seed for change, growth, and transformation in your life, imagine how your life could grow? Nature does not have a consciousness and the ability to create itself. We alone were given this gift. We cannot afford to just sit around and be unconscious of who we are and what we are doing. To do this is to live in stagnation, which in nature is the beginning stage of death. Nature is a mirror and a metaphor for our lives, a subject to reflect on. "Pay attention to the landscape of your life," the inner voice said. What part of your life has been dormant for too long? Pay attention to the places within you that are stagnant. They are blocks to the flow of the abundance that awaits you.

Planting the Seeds

So where do you go from here? Look closely at the landscape of your life. Find the places within that need to grow and change, and plant a seed for that change today. If you want more love in your life, plant a seed and become the love you want. That way you'll always have enough. If you're waiting for the right partner, plant a seed and practice being the perfect partner to yourself. Doing this will help you to give first what you desire most to receive. If you want more money, plant a seed to change your relationship with money. If you want to change your job, travel abroad, or become a writer, plant more seeds. Be conscious of your intentions, about money and other areas of your life, and seek to understand the questions before you go looking for the answers. The answers and the way will be revealed.

If you want to change your life, you must become more conscious of your innermost needs and perhaps do things differently. You cannot ask for circumstances alone to change while you sit passively back and wait for the results. This is your life: no one can do the work for you. You are the artist, so make your life a work of art. This is no easy task, but it is always worth the effort.

Have you ever watched a seed work its tiny stem up from the ground? No matter how hard and resistant the ground above it is, the seed still manages to push through. This is an amazing and miraculous process. So is your life. Whatever you need to push through to get to the other side, you can do it. These are not just words. We have all had to struggle with hardship and adversity. But it is through struggle that we learn to know our strengths and discover our courage.

Do not believe for a minute that you are alone in this process. You are not. You still have much to give and to receive. The fact that you are alive is the only proof you need. It is that simple. You can begin to transform your life by consciously planting at least one seed every day of your life: a seed for change, creativity, love, joy, abundance, or prosperity. See what you can become. You are the gardener of your life. Love and nurture it. Believe in its possibilities.

God will provide the warmth, the sun, and the Light. Work it daily. Start today.

Sixty-Day Prosperity Program

It is said that old habits die hard. To use the information in this book, you need to make conscious choices to change your relationship with money while the information is still fresh in your mind. If you only read this book but do nothing to change your thoughts and actions, you will miss an opportunity to transform your life. To successfully implement meaningful change, particularly change that involves lifelong unconscious behavior, I recommend that you dedicate a minimum of sixty days to creating a new consciousness.

Within the first thirty days, you should begin to see a difference in your level of awareness, and you may even experience a distinct shift in your financial life. However, do not discontinue the program before the end of the sixty-day period, because your mind is likely to revert back to its previous patterns. Studies indicate that patterns of behavior create physical neural patterns in the brain over time. Until new behaviors are firmly established, your mind is naturally inclined to resume old habits. Consequently, the longer you repeat any positive thought or behavior, the more likely it will stick and become an automatic response.

Creating Your Prosperity Program

1. Create a list of everything you are grateful for — your gratitude list.
2. Create a list of all the things that you do not

already possess that you need or want — your wish list.

3. Create a sacred altar in your home consisting of anything that represents what you value most in life and what you seek to manifest. (If you don't already own these things, create a collage with pictures that represent them.) Place a candle on your altar.

4. Spend a minimum of five minutes in the morning and at night before your altar in prayer and meditation. Begin by lighting the candle as a symbol of the Light from within that connects you to Spirit. Read aloud from your gratitude list and give thanks for what you have been given. Read aloud from your wish list and ask that you be shown the way to receiving all that you need. The power of invocation represented by this daily ritual has been used effectively for centuries. As you develop your relationship with Spirit, you will learn the dance of enlightened collaboration.

5. Keep a small tablet with you at all times. Whenever you think or say anything negative about money, whether it is a passing fear or a thought about yourself or someone else, write it down. Catch yourself the minute you say or think anything that contradicts your intention. As you write it down, consciously say to yourself, "This is not what I truly believe, nor does this belief serve my purpose. I will not house this thought in my mind any longer."

6. Try to avoid people who have negative money attitudes and behaviors. Their energy is counterproductive to making positive changes in your life. If it is not possible to avoid them, try asking them to cease expressing their negative thoughts to you.

7. Keep a one hundred dollar bill in your wallet or purse as a reminder of the invisible supply. Try not to spend it. There is more where it came from. This money is a symbol of all that is available to you. Just because you don't have all the money you feel you need at this moment does not mean it won't come. There is an invisible supply of money, and all that you need has been earmarked for you.

8. Practice being generous through acts of conscious giving. Pay attention to the unspoken needs of those around you. Do they need something that you can give — a kind word, a gesture, a smile, a meal? It does not matter what it is. What matters is that you practice knowing and living from a place of abundance.

9. Choose a sacred witness to share this experience with you. Choose someone you trust with your life, and with whom you can share everything and know that you are safe. Ask them to "hold a space" in their heart for you to make your dreams a reality. Only discuss what you are doing with your sacred witness during this transition time.

10. Surrender your fears of lack and limitation. Write a letter to God (or to your friend) and send all your fear on a vacation for sixty days. Don't be surprised, however, if your fear does not come back.

11. Look in the mirror every day and remind yourself that there is more to you than what you see. You are very familiar with this outer reflection of yourself. How well do you know the inside? Take the time in the next sixty days to become more familiar with the inner you. One thing is certain: All of you is well worth knowing.

Lifelong Prosperity

When sixty days have passed, you may or may not have manifested the money or changes you have worked to transform. That does not mean it isn't going to happen. Remember that although we must never be afraid to ask for what we want, we must also remain unattached to the outcome. Ask and release. Stay focused on your path and go about your life. Leave the details to God. This is the hardest part of the lesson, but once you've mastered it, everything else will seem easy. Hold onto your faith like the arm of a fierce friend. In time, you will see changes in yourself and your life that are clear indications of what is yet to come. Along the way, you may encounter people, even friends and family, who challenge your faith and make you feel your efforts are fruitless. They are not. It takes time to become a Magician. Stay on the path and always maintain your connection to Spirit. Live your life with a full heart and do what needs to be done with faith and trust that all is in divine order.

resources and recommended reading

Beckwith, Michael. *40-Day Mind Fast, Soul Feast.* Culver City, Calif.: Agape Press, 2000.

Chopra, Deepak. *The Seven Spiritual Laws of Success.* San Rafael, Calif.: Amber-Allen Publishing and New World Library, 1994.

Gawain, Shatki. *Living in the Light.* Novato, Calif.: New World Library, 1998.

Harvey, Andrew. *The Direct Path: Creating a Journey to the Divine Using the World's Mystical Traditions.* New York: Broadway Books, 2000.

Holmes, Ernest. *How to Change Your Life.* Deerfield, Calif.: Science of Mind Publishing, Health Communications, 1982.

Needleman, Jacob. *Money and the Meaning of Life.* New York: Doubleday, 1991.

Rumi, Jalal Al-Din. *The Illuminated Rumi.* Translation and

commentary by Coleman Barks. New York: Broadway Books, 1997.

Shield, Benjamin and Richard Carlson, eds. *For the Love of God: Handbook for the Spirit.* Novato, Calif.: New World Library, 1997.

Weatherford, Jack. *The History of Money.* New York: Three Rivers Press, 1997.

about the author

Deborah Price is the founder of the Money Coaching Institute, which provides money coaching services to both individuals and businesses. The Money coaching Institute also trains and certifies Money Coaches.

Deborah's experience includes seventeen years in the financial services industry working with firms such as Merrill Lynch, Mass Mutual, Edward Jones, and Robert Thomas Securities. She is a licensed independent financial advisor affiliated with London Pacific Advisors, Inc.

In addition to her work with Money Coaching Institute, Deborah conducts seminars on variety of topics. Her previous books include *Start Investing Online Today* (Adams Media.) She has appeared on numerous radio and television shows, including NBC's *Men Are from Mars, Women Are from Venus Show.* She lives on a vineyard in Healdsburg, California, with her daughter.

To receive a free cassette tape on Money Coaching, register online at: www.money-therapy.com

For information regarding money coaching, seminars or speaking engagements:

Call: (800) 639-0977

Visit her website: www.money-therapy.com

New World Library is dedicated to publishing books, audiocassettes, and videotapes that inspire and challenge us to improve the quality of our lives and our world.

Our books and tapes are available in bookstores everywhere. For a catalog of our complete library of fine books and cassettes, contact:

New World Library
14 Pamaron Way
Novato, CA 94949

Phone: (415) 884-2100
Fax: (415) 884-2199
Or call toll-free (800) 972-6657
Catalog requests: Ext. 50
Ordering: Ext. 52

E-mail: escort@nwlib.com
www.newworldlibrary.com